SO CLOSE TO GLORY

SO CLOSE TO GLORY

THE LIONS IN NEW ZEALAND 1993

Ian McGeechan

with end of tour reflections from Gavin Hastings

Queen Anne Press

in association with

Scottish Life

A QUEEN ANNE PRESS BOOK

© Lennard Associates Ltd 1993

First published in 1993 by
Queen Anne Press, a division of
Lennard Associates Ltd
Mackerye End
Harpenden, Herts AL5 5DR

A catalogue entry is available from the British Library

ISBN 1 85291 532 3

Edited by Caroline North
Design by Cooper Wilson

Printed and bound in Great Britain by
BPCC Hazell Books Ltd
Member of BPCC Ltd

ACKNOWLEDGEMENTS

First and foremost, I would like to thank Scottish Life for their major sponsorship of this book and for all the support
they have given me before, during and after the tour. I am also very grateful for all the tremendous additional
support from Qantas Airways, United Distillers, the Hongkong and Shanghai Banking Corporation and Peter Scott
Knitwear; without such assistance it would not have been possible to have such a glossy production.
On that note I would like to pay special tribute to the excellent photographs from Colin Elsey of Colorsport.
Thanks also to Olympix for their coverage of the first two matches of the tour and to Peter Bush and John Selkirk for
a few additional photos. I would also like to thank Ian Robertson for his help in editing the final manuscript and
Adrian Stephenson for his encouragement throughout the project. Finally, I want to put on record my gratitude to
the army of secretaries who devoted countless hours to transcribing eight weeks of my random thoughts up and down
New Zealand as well as preparing the finished article; to Katie Nicholls in London, to Heather Eliot in Auckland, to
Kerry Grapes in Napier, Bridget MacBeth at the Park Royal Hotel in Wellington and to Christine Li, Angel and Ice
at the Business Centre in the Hong Kong Hilton where I spent a very pleasant week immediately after the tour
finishing the book.

CONTENTS

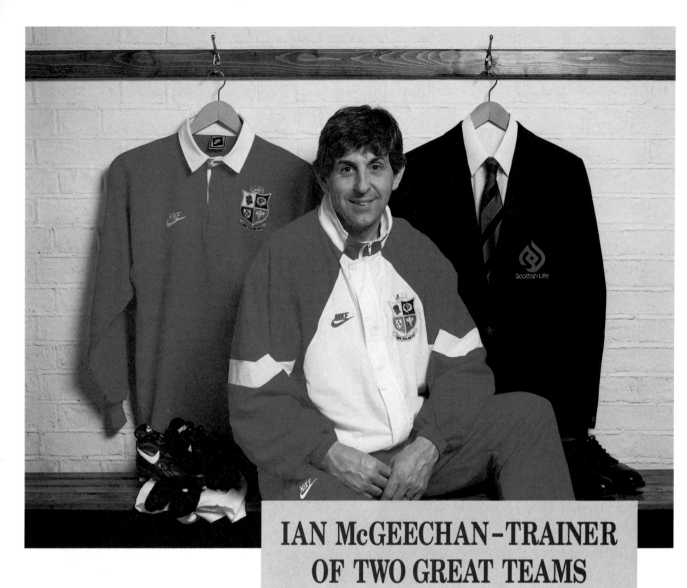

IAN McGEECHAN–TRAINER OF TWO GREAT TEAMS

Training Manager at Scottish Life during the week, Ian McGeechan ensures that the service we offer makes us a hard team to beat.

A recognised rugby guru, Ian is one of the world's most successful rugby coaches. Taking the British Lions to victory in Australia in 1989 and Scotland to the Grand Slam in 1990, he also achieved as a player 32 Scottish caps, and played in eight Lions' tests. And of course, Ian employed all his experience and abilities with the British Lions, as the coach for the 1993 rugby tour of New Zealand.

Accordingly, Ian brings a wealth of training and management skills to our team.

Both in the financial field and on the rugby field, it pays to be trained by the best.

NEW ZEALAND 1993

CORPORATE SUPPORTER OF THE BRITISH LIONS

Pensions &
Mortgages

Scottish Life
THE LIFE TO LEAD

FOREWORD

Lions tours to New Zealand are rare events and have a unique atmosphere. Passion, commitment and sheer rugby ability throughout that country ensure the sternest test of any touring team.

Scottish Life actively supports British rugby already, but with this tour we have a particularly strong link – Ian McGeechan, our Training Manager, was appointed Lions Coach.

The respect that Ian enjoys in the rugby world is legendary and thoroughly deserved, so we were happy that he should take time off "down under" to train the Lions. Good training is invaluable, whether in business or in rugby.

As Corporate Supporters of the British Lions, Scottish Life helped to make the tour possible. Now we are supporting the publication of this book as a record of the tour. It provides a pictorial and statistical source of reference, but it also conveys the intensity of feeling and pure enjoyment of all those who took part.

For the enthusiast, rugby is more than just a game. It enhances the quality of life. In the following pages the experiences of the Lions tourists for a few weeks can be summed up by our slogan "The Life to Lead". I hope you enjoy the book and the memories it leaves.

G. Malcolm Murray
Chief General Manager
Scottish Life

SELECTION AND PLANNING

The tour began in earnest on Saturday 22nd May 1993 in the first match against North Auckland in Whangarei, but as far as I was concerned it started in August 1992. That was when I was appointed the coach of the British Lions along with Dick Best as assistant coach and Geoff Cooke as team manager.

The three of us had a meeting then to discuss in general terms the sort of players we would need for a 13-match tour of New Zealand and we knew we were going to have a very busy schedule during the ensuing seven months, travelling the length and the breadth of Britain and Ireland trying to sort out the cream of British rugby. We were joined by one selector from each of the four Home Unions and in November we had our first joint meeting of the three-man Lions management team plus Derek Morgan of England, David Richards of Wales, Ken Reid of Ireland and Bob Munro of Scotland. Dick Best sat in on selection even though he had no actual vote.

Pre-tour photocall with Geoff Cooke and Dick Best.

We all met again in late February when we were able to compile a nucleus of the key players we knew we would definitely want on the trip, and at that point we also highlighted a group of players from which we reckoned those very tricky highly debatable last dozen players would be added. It is easy to appreciate that it was not very difficult to come up with names like Gavin Hastings, Jeremy Guscott or Martin Bayfield, but it was a lot harder to sort out the front row or the composition of the back row.

I'm pleased to say the tour management team got on well together from the very beginning in the autumn of 1992. I've known Geoff for a long long time. Indeed, he insists that he taught me all that I know about coaching, a leg-pulling reference (I think) to our links some 20 years ago when I was playing for Yorkshire and Geoff was coach. Little did we realise then…

We were both schoolmasters in Leeds and lived within a couple of miles of each other. I would be wrong to suggest we knew one another well, but we did have regular contact and rugby was the bond. The subsequent pursuit of different paths restricted our meetings, though when Geoff became England's manager in November 1987, in succession to my old friend Mike Weston, the links – and the rivalry – were happily renewed.

It was necessary, too, to set out guidelines – a job definition, if you like – for the range of individual management responsibilities. Plainly it was my duty to prepare the side, establish training routines, present tactical schemes, analyse all aspects of play, including the likely opposition, and, the most important consideration of all, lead the debate on selection.

It goes without saying that this Lions tour, like every previous Lions tour with which I have been associated, was not simply a case of writing down the names of 30 automatic selections. Lions selection creates the basis for all talking-points, informed and otherwise. I've been constantly fascinated by what I'm told by those outside the selection processes and by what I read, hear and see written or spoken by those pundits who present the game, and all it entails, to the public at large. I've no wish to condemn with faint praise but I have to say that while some do it well, others do not.

Suffice to say the Lions selectors spent a great deal of time and energy over seven long months discussing and debating the make-up of the tour party before finalising it at the end of a six-hour meeting at the Edwardian Hotel at Heathrow near London on Monday 22nd March. We knew the sort of players we wanted to take on the New Zealanders on their home territory in their winter conditions, accepting the current strengths of their national and even top provincial sides. We knew the style of play we wanted and after agonising for six hours, with most of that time spent choosing the forwards, we were ready to name our squad of 30. It would be foolish to pretend that every decision on every position was unanimous because that was not the case, but I can say that at no time on any position did we need to resort to a vote. It was all done amicably by consensus.

Without betraying any confidences, there were certainly differences of opinion on a handful of the final decisions. As far as I was concerned I went in to that final selection meeting with a list of 25 key players around whom I

The touring party, plus mascot, assembles at the Oatlands Park Hotel near Weybridge.
LEFT TO RIGHT:
Nick Popplewell, Peter Wright, Robert Jones, Dick Best, Stuart Barnes, Mike Teague, Tony Underwood, Dean Richards, Ieuan Evans, Rory Underwood, Wade Dooley, Rob Andrew, Scott Hastings, Martin Bayfield, Geoff Cooke, Dewi Morris, Andy Reed, Gavin Hastings, Damian Cronin, Richard Webster, Ian McGeechan, Mick Galwey, Jeremy Guscott, Brian Moore, Paul Burnell, Will Carling, Ian Hunter, Scott Gibbs, Ben Clarke, Anthony Clement, Dr James Robson, Jason Leonard, Ken Milne, Peter Winterbottom, Kevin Murphy.

hoped to build the eventual Test team. All 25 were selected and I was perfectly satisfied with the tour party.

At the time, two days after Ireland had comprehensively beaten England, it may have seemed very tough on the Irish to find only two people selected whilst England contributed over half of the 30-man squad, but we picked everyone not on the basis of one international but on form over an entire season. We also took into account the previous experience of all these players, their 1993 form – even their pre-1993 form – their character, their ability to act under intense pressure in the international arena and their capability in the cauldron of New Zealand rugby to absorb and soak up fierce physical punishment.

Of course I have every sympathy with the Irish, but if it is any consolation not only did they provide the first two replacements of the tour, but they had several other players who only narrowly missed out on selection. There was a great deal of discussion about the make-up of the back row, both individually and collectively, and it wasn't easy choosing the half-backs or the front row.

Furthermore, this selection was to do a specific job, playing a particular style of rugby against specific opposition in New Zealand. These would not have been exactly the same 30 players we would have chosen to go on a Lions tour in 1993 to Australia or South Africa, and I hope I have made it absolutely clear that the announcement of the 30 names came at the end of a painstaking process.

Judging by much of the press reaction the following day, you might have thought we had rushed into a room, thrown 50 names into a lucky bag and pulled out 30. This is not what happened, and I would, by and large, be happy to defend that original selection because back in March we believed it to be the right choice. It was very frustrating to read on the Tuesday in some papers that we had made a few very bad selections for the sort of game we would be playing in New Zealand. Now, with all respect to those journalists, how did they know what sort of a game them would be playing? I knew precisely the sort of game I wanted the Lions to play, and it was certainly not the sort of style any one of the four Home Unions had played in the Five Nations Championship.

I make this as a general comment because I must say that over the years I have enjoyed a very good rapport with the majority of the media. The Scottish press, TV and radio may be a disparate bunch, but they are a relatively small unit, easy to approach and sympathetic in the main. Come to the UK and Irish media as a whole, though, and it is a different ball game. On a Lions tour, I discourage national factions; that's not the name of the game and, given the platform day by day for press conferences and TV and radio interviews, I use it. This is the Lions. It is not Scotland or England, or Wales or Ireland. It is the Lions, an area of activity and responsibility about which I've very firm views.

What I said in London before departure and in Auckland on arrival can be summed up as follows: "The concept of the Lions is something that feels natural. It is right. Even though the modern game is evolving in different ways, I think it would be very sad if there wasn't a place for Lions tours. Happily, they are on the schedule until at least the year 2009."

All good intentions to note down my thoughts about the 101 things that happen every day while touring did not last. There is, of course, the routine and the repetition, the need to ensure that the little things are right and, at all times, that the players are aware of what management want to do. Each group of players offers a different challenge. People and personalities, thank goodness, are not the same. I try to tell everyone simply, directly, what I seek as a coach; what I expect. I don't shout or swear or thump the table but I do appeal to competitive instincts of pride, performance, of the need of each to work with and for the other.

I make no differentiation, be it the Lions, the World XV, Scotland or whatever. Games-playing is about maximising talents, being flexible, being aware. Awareness and adaptability were my theme words in that first week in Paihia – and continued to be as we covered the whole of the best rugby-playing country in the world, from the Bay of Islands in the far north to Invercargill in the south.

Arguably the most difficult decision we had to make was the choice of captain. It is no secret that it was a straight choice between Gavin Hastings, the captain of Scotland for just one season, and the highly successful Will Carling, captain of England for five years which included two Grand Slams and the final of the World Cup. If we had had to announce the Lions captain in August it is 99 per cent certain we would have chosen Will, and it would have been a unanimous decision. Yet, curiously enough, the two big deciding factors in

Captains three: Ieuan
Evans, Gavin Hastings
and Will Carling.

Gavin's favour the following March were both in place in August 1992. He had been on a previous Lions tour, and a hugely successful one at that, and he had a great deal of experience playing rugby in New Zealand over a six-year period. Will, through no fault of his own, drew a blank on both counts.

Picking the right captain was vitally important to the tour and a whole host of factors had to be taken into account. Gavin had an enormous number of plus points and in listing some of the most crucial I am simply stating his case and I am not in any way making a direct comparison with Will. Above all, he was certain, barring injury, of his place in the Test side, which has not always been the case with Lions captains in the past.

As I have already mentioned, he played in New Zealand for three weeks with Scotland during the 1987 World Cup and, equally significantly, he played very well then and throughout the Scotland tour to New Zealand in 1990. He was such an outstanding player that he instantly became and has remained a rugby hero in the eyes of the whole New Zealand rugby public. They do not toss out such generous accolades lightly, and he has always been highly admired and respected as a great rugby player by the Kiwis, all the more so for his magnificent deeds in their country. He also played really well in club rugby in the Auckland area for a while immediately after the 1987 World Cup, and he underlined his genius again in 1992 playing for the World XV during the New Zealand Centenary celebrations.

As a direct consequence of all his exploits on the field of play, Gavin has enjoyed a very high profile in New Zealand. He fully understood and appreciated the intense rugby environment in New Zealand, which is unparalleled anywhere else in the world and would have to come as something of a shock to anyone unfamiliar with it on a first visit.

A high profile, it has to be said, is not everything. Hitler had a high profile. But Gavin has always been immensely popular "Down Under" since his first visit in 1987. That devotion could only make captaining the Lions very much easier for him. Part of his appeal is that he is a very laid-back, gregarious and friendly individual. He does not flap or panic in pressure situations. He is eminently approachable and very good at dealing with all the players as individuals.

Behind his amiable persona there is a man of steel who is a most astute rugby tactician and someone who takes rugby very seriously. A rugby child, as it were, of the 90s, he is fully aware of and particularly adept at dealing with the responsibilities of the modern player and captain. He is very good and relaxed with the media and coasts comfortably through the seemingly incessant press conferences and radio and television interviews. He has genuine credibility with the players from all four Home Unions, both as a player and as a person.

And even if all that had not made him an ideal candidate for the captaincy of the British Lions, he also had the previous experience of touring with the Lions in Australia in 1989. He was an absolutely key member of that victorious side in the three Tests, and the insight into touring he gained with the 1989 Lions was an invaluable advantage. That tour, it should be pointed out, was only the second time the Lions had won a Test series this century.

Against that very impressive list of credentials, Will Carling was unavoidably deficient in two key areas: he had missed the 1989 Lions tour through injury and he had never set foot in New Zealand. For all his other many attributes, and accepting that he has been far and away the most successful captain of England in the history of the game – indeed, one of the most successful international rugby captains ever of any country in the world – I believe we were right to make Gavin Hastings the captain of the Lions.

The party worked well together from the start and I was particularly pleased with the natural authority of Gavin Hastings, which was a focal point for everyone. The old soldiers Dean Richards and Brian Moore, with whom I'd worked so closely and successfully in 1989, also set a fine example in that opening week when, to be honest, our prime intention was to get into the first match against North Auckland as quickly as was decently possible.

I am a fervent supporter of Lions tours and I really hope that, as the international player's schedule becomes ever more crowded, the powers that be somehow manage to keep a slot every four years for a 13-match tour. If the Home Unions are in any doubt they should ask the 1993 Lions. Ask the 1989 or 1983 tourists or, for that matter, any surviving Lions from any previous tour what they think. Ask the New Zealand, South African and Australian rugby unions. I am confident the response would be 100 per cent in favour. I enjoyed immensely my Lions tours in 1974 and 1977 as a player, and equally I relished every moment of the massive challenge as coach in 1989 and 1993.

My views about the value of Lions tours have been widely publicised. Those views have not changed one iota since I was first involved back in 1974 when I toured South Africa. I make no excuse for repeating that the concept of the Lions is important in the education of British and Irish players. The Lions helped cement friendships and break down some perceived barriers. Without doubt, to my way of thinking, the Five Nations Championship since 1989 has been better for the Lions tour to Australia. Remember that there had been no tour previously for six years and domestic attitudes had hardened, not least, I imagine, because of World Cup rivalries and some less than enthralling encounters between Scotland and England.

Players can become isolated if directed solely down national lines. That's not a bad thing in itself, but the Lions concept enables those involved to step away from the narrow world and take a broader view. I think that is extremely important, quite apart from also being the pinnacle of any playing career. It would be a great shame – I speak as a player and as a coach – if that opportunity ceased to be available to the next generation of international players. For my part I learned a hell of a lot on Lions tours. They are different to anything else that a rugby player experiences. But enough tub-thumping. Back to our plans for demonstrating that New Zealand did not hold all the aces.

With the Lions in New Zealand, a country where rugby, no matter all the other diversions, is the top sport, we had to look hard and fast at our own priorities and perceptions of the game. Day after day I was telling players to forget about what happened at home – tactics, refereeing, pace and style, the sheer physical robustness of it all. It was, I said, up to us to adapt. We were in new Zealand and we had to do what they did. Quickly... quickly... don't moan. Adapt... adapt. At the team meetings, on the bus, in private conversations, I stressed: "Get the mental attitude right and some of the physical attributes we have can come to the fore. Be flexible and remember that nothing but the best of the talents we possess will do."

Already thinking of New Zealand: a casual stroll on the croquet lawn before departure.

On the tarmac and all
set to go.

EARLY SUCCESS... AT A COST

New Zealand's weather at its most perverse greeted us on that first Sunday morning. Our destination was Paihia in the Bay of Islands – an idyllic resort for the boating fraternity, the golfers and those anxious to learn about the country's history, for it was just down the road that the Treaty of Waitangi was signed in 1840. Waitangi, I am told, means Weeping Waters in Maori. Weep they did, too. The overnight storm brought down power lines. There were electricity cuts and we ate our first breakfast by candlelight. The supposedly tranquil bay, the home of hundreds of islands, was a raging sea. Trees were bent in the wind and the rain lashed down. For us, outside training would be a waste of time. Instead we had a gym session some ten miles away in Kawakawa, a town, I was reminded, which is home for the numerous members of the Going family. Sid would be coaching North Auckland, our opponents in the first match, and I'd not the slightest doubt that our various training routines, tactical rehearsals and likely game plan would be quickly transmitted to the opposition.

The first outdoor session in New Zealand at the Bay of Islands – a run along the beach, some exercises and a few shuttles just to get rid of the journey.

I do like to work privately where possible once or twice before a major match. But I don't, at least I hope I don't, make too much of a fuss about it. Private training sessions permit a coach to attend to the fine tuning, to the detail, something which is not always possible or politic in the normal scheme of things. Remember, New Zealand is a country where crowds – yes, crowds – turn out in force to watch training, a phenomenon not known at home in my experience.

In fact, in that first week we were always in the open in full public view at either Kerikeri or Kawakawa and did not go behind closed doors until we got down to North Harbour, which, geographically, is Auckland. There it was suggested to us that we should train at the New Zealand Royal Navy establishment at Devonport. That, obviously, was a secure area with restricted admittance, and that's where we went.

I worked the players hard in that opening week and, apart from the odd injury niggle here and there, it went well enough. Martin Bayfield had a hamstring twinge and Tony Underwood didn't train for a couple of days but, by and large, I got through all the routines I had in mind. Geoff Cooke's deep knowledge and experience as a coach and the sharp insight (and tongue) of Dick Best ensured that we kept up to scratch.

Technically, there were law changes to consider, and the likely interpretations by referees and, of course, the opposition. I was one of the national coaches who attended the March meeting in Hong Kong where we produced a paper on how we saw things. The IRB were given a copy and, to a great extent, most of the ideas of the coaches were incorporated in one form or another in their revision of the laws at the annual IB meeting in April. The object in the broadest terms was to encourage continuity, to promote handling skills and to make the ball more freely available. We also pleaded for universal interpretations, but I doubt that we would agree amongst ourselves what that constituted anyway, and we were in for some disappointments in that regard during the Lions tour.

Dewi Morris dressed to kill during a bit of relaxation at the Bay of Islands.

For all that I have never been one to carp about referees. A player's duty is to play to the whistle, to adjust as quickly as possible to what he considers the match official requires and, in extreme cases to follow the example of the opposition, especially the hosts. Grumbling will get you nowhere in a match.

As to those law changes, Law 24 was the prime issue. Players joining or rejoining a ruck or maul must do so from behind their offside line – the line through the hindmost foot of the team – not the line of the ball. Furthermore, if a player catches a kick on the full from an opponent and a maul forms immediately, his team will have the put in to any ensuing scrum. There were also some tidying up bits and pieces relating to penalty awards, free kicks, restarts if the ball is kicked dead and the reminder that the restriction which states that a dropped goal cannot be scored from a free kick also applied to scrums taken in lieu of free kicks.

I was determined that this Lions squad should be aware of all the pitfalls. I am not interested in excuses, only performance: positive performance. It might be human nature for the pessimist to fear the worst so that he will never be disappointed, but I have been fascinated through the years that so-called knowledgeable critics dwell only on the down-side, on the things that teams have not done well. Failure is a popular word with the knocking brigade. Little if any credit is given to the opposition who, no matter what you may have planned or hoped to do, are there to stop you doing exactly that. You may still win even if they succeed in putting the block on – but to do so, you will have had a very tight contest and possibly will have produced a not particularly edifying spectacle.

At the outset, we chatted through the schedule and where and when, for example, Gavin would play. We came to the fairly surprising conclusion that a case could be made for leaving him out of the opening match. Now, I regard myself as a traditionalist, and although I played a straight bat at the press announcement, I have to say that originally I would have expected the tour captain to appear in the opening match.

Gavin was approached, he agreed to stand down and so he got no further than the bench for the opening match – or, at least, that is how we planned it. In the event he was on the field immediately before half-time, to replace Ian

Hunter, who had been playing on the right wing. This first bad injury was an acid taste of things to come. Ian dislocated his right shoulder when somehow his hand got entangled in the shorts of a large Tongan wing. If Ian told the world that his opponent, and All Black trialist, had two names, two ages, and had been living and working in new Zealand illegally, he would be right. The irony was not lost on us, though, for Ian, having had a year interrupted incessantly by injury, found this episode was yet another instance of a foul run of bad luck.

Within 48 hours, Ian was on his way home. He handled his disappointment well and, I gather, dealt shrewdly with the media when, inevitably, interviews were sought on the Sunday morning after the match and we made our decision to send for Richard Wallace, Ireland's wing, as a replacement. We brought Ian to New Zealand because we felt his physical strength and attacking skills would serve as a further weapon in the variety of offensive plans we had in mind. It was a bitter blow to lose him almost before the tour had begun.

All conversations in that first week seemed to suggest that New Zealand were conditioned to anticipating a large, experienced pack which would attempt to lay down the law and that we would spend part of every match trying to steam-roller in from ten yards or less. I was happy to let them think that, mostly because I knew differently. The time to declare our true intentions, to reveal our speed, natural guile and immense ability out wide would come soon enough. I knew, too, that the midfield would embarrass the best-organised

The teams within the team. Each training group produced their own names kindly made into T-shirts by Dewi Morris's company. No need to guess the team which included Scott Gibbs!

defences. Not, of course, that there is anything wrong with paying acute attention to defence. Organise it sensibly and matches which otherwise might have been lost will be won.

From an early point it was made clear to the players that everyone would play

in the opening two matches and, very soon, we expanded that to include two matches apiece before Test match selection dominated our thoughts and preparation. I had a good idea of most of the players I wanted in that Test team to oppose the All Blacks on 12th June but there were still several players in with a good chance of making the side as I had to pick on current form and go for the best combinations. For those

Discussing, with Gavin and Dick Best, our hopes for a good performance against North Auckland. Gavin was happy to put the side first and remain on the sidelines for this opening game.

RIGHT The tour begins for real and Stuart Barnes rather than Gavin Hastings leads out the team for the first game.

not in that provisional line-up – and I was keeping my own counsel on that – there was still every incentive. Above all, in a touring situation, form is the first consideration. There have to be others, including experience, competitiveness, application of skills in tight moments and consistency. But at the top of the list is form.

It is not always possible for a coach to be fair in allotting equal opportunity, especially when injuries intervene. But I do believe in letting all concerned know what is in my mind and why, and, of course, updating situations when circumstances change. What with one thing and another I seemed to be revising my options and ideas on a daily basis.

If the injury to Ian Hunter concentrated the minds, our resolve could hardly have been stronger in the following two weeks. There were useful victories over North Auckland and North Harbour, a quite startling match of highs and lows against the Maoris and a bread-and-butter win against Canterbury, who faded after a bright start.

North Auckland first, and a 30–17 win. I expected our scrummaging to be workmanlike rather than overpowering became our emphasis had been laid on contact work at the breakdown phases to produce continuity rather than set-piece play at this early stage of the tour. But a win is important to start with. You spend weeks preparing and training but this was achieved under match pressure. Here was something we could build upon. Cards, so to speak, had been marked – none better than by the loose forwards and our fliers out wide.

For this first match of the tour we appointed Stuart Barnes as captain for the day, a responsibility which momentarily left even that talkative soul at a loss for words. He played against North Auckland in 1992 on the England "B" tour, which he also led, and I had every confidence that we had chosen well.

Old rival and North Auckland coach Sid Going, bless him, grumbled a little

The first try of the game goes to North Auckland and we realise we are in for a hell of a tour.

afterwards about our line-out play and offside at ruck and maul. For my part, I was surprised to see how often New Zealand players went to ground unpunished. It appeared that as long as the intent was to keep the ball alive, not to kill it, there was licence to ignore the precise terms of the law book. But I kept quiet and mention it now only to indicate what match conditions referees permitted. I had no quarrels in the broadest sense. When in Rome, do as the Romans do. When in Whangarei…

We allowed their hooker, Doug Te Puni, to escape after ten minutes or so on one of those sweeping support raids which covered 60 yards, starting left and finishing right to score the first try of the tour. The Lions answered with tries by Jeremy Guscott and Scott Hastings – a three-minute salvo of 12 points was better than any words of mine and indicated that the 1993 Lions meant business and that there was ammunition to back up our intent. And let me make it quite clear that these were both pretty good tries. For the first Clement and Barnes created the space for Guscott, who glided through from halfway for a spectacular score. Next Robert Jones kicked over his shoulder towards the left-hand touch. Underwood was in pursuit at 200 mph and the full-back got into a tangle. Scott Hastings was alongside for the try, and with 26 minutes gone I suddenly felt better.

North Auckland did quickly pull back one try, but after half-time, the team having resettled after the injury to Hunter, the Lions were back in charge. When Ben Clarke was held at the line, the attacks multiplied. Another attacking scrum allowed Clarke to pick up, Robert Jones used the blind side and Clement scored for Gavin Hastings to convert. Incidentally, although Gavin was on the field, Barnes, who had kicked the first-half penalty goal, remained in charge as captain. We eased off at 25–12 and paid the penalty when North Auckland ran in a third try, this time by Troy Going. What with the anthem having been sung by Adrian Going and with Charles Going in midfield, there were lots of "Goings" on before the Lions came back in the final minutes. North Auckland bravely ran everything under pressure. Down the ball went and Rory Underwood was put in at the corner by Scott Hastings. At 30–17 I was happy – not delirious, perhaps, but certainly happy enough.

Ben Clarke takes up the New Zealand challenge with a typically aggressive drive, supported by Mick Galwey, Andy Reed and Peter Wright.

For the second match of the tour we played all 15 of the players who did not play in the first game and this meant that for the second time in a few days we fielded a team which, with a couple of exceptions, had not played a competitive match for well over a month. Taking that into consideration it was very satisfying to beat one of the top provinces in New Zealand in such a convincing manner.

To accommodate the huge crowd the venue was switched from North Harbour's own ground to the Commonwealth Games Stadium at Mount Smart, which is a tremendous setting for rugby. I had expected this encounter to be tougher than the North Auckland opener because North Harbour were a leading First Division side. They also had the huge advantage of having participated in the Super-10 competition, which featured top provincial sides from New Zealand, Australia and South Africa.

Analysing video evidence of their 1993 form I could see they had a good pack, strong centres in the All Black pairing of Bunce and Little and good wings. I felt we had been a little slow in securing control in the opening match and I stressed to the team the importance of making a really good start against North Harbour. The players certainly seemed to take this on board because in the first 20 minutes we hardly put a foot wrong and notched up two tries to reward the team for all their hard work.

To prepare for these early games during the developing stages of the tour I concentrated mostly on the loose play for the forwards and the basic running and handling skills for the backs. It is impossible with 30 players from four different countries playing four different styles of rugby to achieve perfection in every single phase of play in a fortnight, so I focused on a few key areas and left other important facets until later. I did not work that intensively on scrummaging or a myriad of line-out variations because I knew I could build that in later in the trip as the Test matches approached. I began with general organisation and discipline both in attack and defence. I got the backs running at the right angles, working at real pace and perfecting fast, accurate passing so we could whip the ball out to the wings faster than any of our opponents. I believed we had real match-winners on the wing in Ieuan Evans and the two Underwood brothers, and we had to get the ball to them rapidly.

I was confident that all four centres could create space to unleash our wings and from set-piece play that half-overlap could also be conjured by Gavin Hastings and Anthony Clement joining the line from full-back. I was also satisfied that I had two sets of half-backs in any combination to complement the threequarters. Both scrum-halves could take the pressure off the backs with fast, sniping breaks and both were good kickers of the ball.

Both Rob Andrew and Stuart Barnes were fully capable of varying their play – kicking tactically, breaking in midfield and linking with the forwards or the centres – and unleashing the back division at the right time. So early on I did not weigh down the backs with a string of set moves but preferred to rely on their natural ability and real speed of thought and deed to make the running and the tries. We also organised our defence so that throughout the tour it would always be very difficult for the opposition to score tries against the Lions.

As for the pack, I tended to concentrate on the loose play in the belief that by our sheer size and strength and inherent skill we would be good enough to perform perfectly adequately in the set pieces. With a lot of help from Dick Best, we worked on keeping up the momentum of every attack and the continuity. This meant loads of speed and stamina work in training, driving into a succession of pads, to ensure the play was tight and the forwards were there in numbers. I emphasised right through the tour the need to arrive at the breakdown really quickly and in numbers. The first four or five to reach the breakdown had to react rapidly to the situation, and whether they were backs or forwards they had to secure possession instantly.

Dick and I worked on body positions at rucks and mauls to get all our players lower so that they were in the most dynamic driving positions to bind together and spreadeagle the opposition. That could only be achieved if we were at the breakdown first, in greater numbers, in the correct driving position and with the greater sense of urgency. I stressed to the whole squad the need to win not just second-phase possession but third, fourth, fifth and sixth phase as well. This was to be the Lions style of forward play. It was undoubtedly a change of emphasis from the way most forwards think in Britain, but it is the way they play in New Zealand and Australia and we had to match them.

What we found frustrating in the North Harbour match and in many of the other games was the disregard shown by the referees at the breakdown for the law which says that at a tackle the third man up should stay on his feet. The general feeling in New Zealand seemed to be that if the follow-up players hit the deck and bodies began to pile up it was perfectly permissible as long as they were all genuinely trying to be positive, attempting to keep the ball alive and keep the game going. That may sound all right in theory, but it is emphatically not what the law book allows and it was all very confusing.

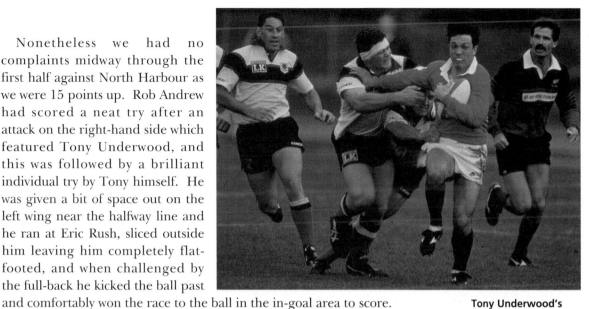

Nonetheless we had no complaints midway through the first half against North Harbour as we were 15 points up. Rob Andrew had scored a neat try after an attack on the right-hand side which featured Tony Underwood, and this was followed by a brilliant individual try by Tony himself. He was given a bit of space out on the left wing near the halfway line and he ran at Eric Rush, sliced outside him leaving him completely flat-footed, and when challenged by the full-back he kicked the ball past and comfortably won the race to the ball in the in-goal area to score.

Tony Underwood's electric pace startled North Harbour on more than one occasion.

With a penalty from Gavin Hastings as well it looked as if we were heading for a big win, but our concentration lapsed early in the second half and they scored a converted try and two penalties which suddenly closed the gap to 15–13. To make matters worse we had one unfortunate incident when Dean Richards injured Frank Bunce at a ruck. The simple fact is that Bunce should have been penalised by the referee immediately for holding the ball on the ground at the ruck in front of North Harbour's posts, but amazingly, he wasn't. Dean then tried to ruck the ball clear quite aggressively and he was penalised when his boot made contact with Bunce's head. Mayhem broke out and Dean ended up with an injured jaw and left the field. It was the only unpleasant

One of the few unsavoury moments of the tour, as the players take the law into their own hands and Dean Richards ends up with a very sore jaw.

incident in the first half of the tour, and it could have been avoided if the referee had done his job and penalised Bunce instantly.

Unfortunately, the line-out was a shambles and the referee penalised us so often that our jumpers had a miserable afternoon. The penalty count against us was quite staggering. In consequence it was gratifying that, with all the ball North Harbour won, we comfortably kept them in check most of the time. The midfield backs – Rob Andrew, Will Carling and Scott Gibbs – tackled superbly and our defensive organisation was excellent.

Richard Webster's impressive try against North Harbour demonstrates the drive and commitment of the team against very good opposition.

Fortunately, in the last quarter of the game we regained control and scored two more tries. Ieuan Evans sprinted through for one and then Richard Webster, who had come on as a replacement for Dean Richards, collected a loose ball following a drive by the Lions and surged forward to storm over the line and score between the posts with a little bit of help from his friends. We finished strongly, and at such an early stage of the tour and against such tough opposition this was a first-class victory.

There were several pleasing aspects in what was a good all-round performance. I was very happy with our defensive play, particularly with that of the loose forwards, Winterbottom, Richards and Webster, the half-backs, Morris and Andrew, and the centres, Carling and Gibbs. Tony Underwood injected real speed into everything he did and I was delighted with Martin Bayfield's play in the line-out. Equally significantly, everything we did in attack was executed at real pace and the only blemish was our difficulty in coming to terms with the referee. His interpretations were very different from what we had expected and from what we understood him to have laid down at our briefing meeting with him before the match. But this was a worthwhile lesson for the players, because we had talked about just such a situation occurring and how it was essential to adapt to the referee, to listen to him and to do exactly what he wanted so we could get on with playing rugby.

We accepted that our problems with referees would probably not end with the North Harbour match but we set off for Wellington in a good frame of mind with two wins from two games, and pleased that all 30 players had had a game. The decision was taken to continue this policy by playing all 30 players again in the next two games, which was not only good for everyone's morale but also important for the selection committee, because we needed to experiment with several different combinations before we would be in a position to finalise our team for the First Test.

On previous Lions tours in which I had been involved it had seemed relatively easy to work out the midweek "dirt-trackers" side and the Saturday Test side, but I felt it was essential this time to be seen to be giving every single player a fair crack of the whip, especially as I had left Britain with only a few preconceived ideas of the make-up of the Test side and half a dozen positions were still in the melting-pot. I was well aware that in several positions there was bound to be intense competition for places with very little to choose between the candidates. I could see no absolutely clear-cut division at half-back or in the centre, and there was not a great deal to choose between the wings or the front-row players.

It was also clear to me that the final composition of the Test match back row was going to be a very delicate balancing act. Of course, the big problem for the 1993 Lions party was the length of the tour. Until the 1983 tour which was reduced to 18 games, all previous such tours to New Zealand had consisted of well over 20 matches spread over at least three months. In the old days the team had the best part of six weeks to prepare for the First Test whereas on the 1993 tour exactly six weeks after the opening match in North Auckland we played the final Test. This presented huge problems for me as coach and for the whole tour party. We were trying to weld together 30 players from four different countries in roughly half the time that previous Lions coaches had had throughout the 20th century on major tours to New Zealand and South Africa.

Admittedly, the only previous experience I had as coach was of a short 13-match tour when I took the Lions to Australia in 1989, but that trip has to be put into context. Outside the international team the only outstanding sides in Australia are New South Wales and Queensland, which meant that the majority of our games in 1989 were nowhere near the standard of the big provincial matches in New Zealand in 1993. There was nothing in midweek in Australia to compare with North Harbour, Canterbury, Hawke's Bay or Waikato, so it had not presented quite the formidable challenge of 1993.

Immediately after our First Test defeat in Christchurch, the former great All Black wing Stu Wilson said on radio that he thought the Lions must have been insane and certifiable to accept such a punitive fixture list. I sympathise with the point he was making, but he was being quite unrealistic if he expected us to tell the New Zealand council the fixtures were too hard and we would appreciate a few more games against second-division opposition. Furthermore, as coach, I was never at any stage consulted about the fixtures; it was a *fait accompli*.

Stu Wilson should know that when the All Blacks come to the UK they will no longer be given easy matches. Those days are gone forever. Oxford and Cambridge Universities, the Combined Services and other relative "soft touches" are a thing of the past, and in England and Scotland in late 1993, for example, they would meet the top divisions. They would come up against only the top 60 or 70 players in the whole of those two countries and then finish up playing Scotland, England and the Barbarians, which would be virtually the British Lions, on three successive Saturdays. Are the All Blacks insane or certifiable to accept that itinerary? The answer is no. It was only right that the Lions should play the top four provincial sides in New Zealand on this tour, and I have no major complaint about the itinerary.

That does not mean to suggest for one minute that I did not fully appreciate what an awesome challenge it was going to be, but I genuinely felt from the outset that we were up to it. I never anticipated an unbeaten tour, but I certainly had high hopes of a very successful tour. Funnily enough, when I saw the itinerary for the first time I picked out the New Zealand Maori game as probably the toughest of our opening four matches, and so it turned out.

Judged by any standards this was a wonderful game of rugby and it was one of those occasions which nobody who played in it will ever forget. It provided one of the great recoveries as the Lions fought back from a seemingly impossible position at half-time to a brilliant victory at the end. It was a remarkable game. The Maoris were all over us in the first half, but a complete transformation in the second allowed the Lions to gradually take control.

We had a strong hint of what was to come in that first half right from the start. We kicked off and immediately put a lot of pressure on them. We won the ball and hoisted a high kick to the posts. Three of the Lions followed up and caught the full-back, Doyle, as he took the ball perilously near to his goal-line. I was sitting in the stand rubbing my hands in delight in the belief that we were about to open the scoring in the first minute. But it was not to be because we allowed him to stay on his feet and in our enthusiasm we piled in and we were penalised for going over the top. The Maoris whacked the penalty downfield, won the line-out and sent another raking kick deep into our 22, where they then camped for the next quarter of an hour.

We managed to clear our lines quite regularly but they usually won the next line-out on their own throw and were once again control, driving at us for all they were worth. They had seized the initiative and we were subjected to a very painful 40 minutes. They piled on the pressure as they sensed that we were thoroughly uncomfortable having to play the game on the back foot, on the retreat, in deep defence. They took the lead with two good tries which left us with a lot of ground to make up. First, they hoisted a kick into the glaring sun and Gavin Hastings lost track of the flight of the ball. Their wing, Hirini, collected the loose ball and ran 20 yards to score. Then their forwards managed to maintain their momentum and, after winning good possession from the loose on three occasions in quick succession, they scored another try. Add the two conversions and two penalties and we were on the wrong end of a 20-point hiding.

It could have been even worse because shortly before half-time, when we were on the attack in their 22, we lost possession and the Maoris launched a

Still coming to terms with the line-out interpretation in New Zealand.

major counter-attack in double-quick time. They had half a dozen players inter-passing and in support and I was very relieved that our players realised instantly that this was a real crisis situation and made superhuman efforts to cover. I think this was the turning-point of the match. At least half a dozen players sprinted back and rattled in seven or eight desperate, but crucial, tackles to stop a score which would have made it 27–0 and I don't think the Lions would have been able to pull that back. There were several heroes in that sweeping movement but I must single out Dewi Morris, who made two magnificent tackles, and Rory Underwood, who made one.

At half-time Gavin told the team not to panic and emphasised the need to win some good possession up front, use it well, play the game we wanted to play and, with the slight wind behind us, keep the ball in play. We had learned in the first half how difficult the game can be if the opposition are dictating the throw at the line-out. However, at the end of 20 minutes of pressurised, controlled and disciplined rugby all we had pulled back was one penalty from Gavin Hastings.

Then the whole complexion of the match changed in a trice with two brilliant pieces of inspirational play from Ieuan Evans. All our hard work at Paihia and in Auckland, when we had concentrated on contact work, second-phase possession and speed to the breakdown, paid off. From a line-out we drove into the middle of the field, won the ball and whipped it out to Ieuan. He left his opposite wing for dead and then accelerated outside the full-back at real pace to score a glorious try in the corner.

Almost from the kick-off the Maoris won the ball and tried a little chip kick over the top. Ieuan raced back to cover it, scooped the ball off his toes and slipped a pass to Gavin. The backs moved into overdrive on the counter-attack and, running straight back at the Maoris, we created an overlap for Rory Underwood to score a superb try. Gavin converted both to cut the leeway to 20–17 with ten minutes left.

All of a sudden the horrors of the first half were no more than a distant memory and we were now playing with real confidence. We won another line-out and again drove into the middle of the field. We won the ruck and Stuart Barnes switched back down the blind side where we had a three against one overlap. Gavin Hastings joined the line at pace, sold a dummy, cut inside beating two players and crashed straight through the full-back's tackle to stretch over the line and score a real captain's winning try.

There were still a few minutes remaining and the Maoris came thundering back with two great attacks, but we simply tackled everything that moved and held on for a dramatic win. We had won an exceptional game and had guaranteed that everyone would now take the Lions seriously. Our forwards raised the pace of the game in the second half and started to win good set-piece possession as well as very good loose ball. The backs ran with enormous

An important captain's try from Gavin which secured victory against the Maoris.

confidence and showed quite conclusively that they would be a handful for any and every team in New Zealand.

We also learned one important scrummaging lesson against the Maoris about the whole New Zealand approach to the scrum. As the two packs go down the New Zealanders make a really big "hit" as the front rows lock together. Instead of staying static at that point as we would normally do in Britain, they keep the legs pumping and they try to drive forward. At exactly the same time as they make this hit and edge forward, the scrum-half rolls the ball into the scrum, usually at or even just behind his own hooker's feet! We acknowledged that we had to be ready for that initial hit as the scrums went down and the front rows collided, and we needed to be very tight and in a good, low, driving position.

The other main point to come out of the North Harbour and Maori matches was our approach to rucks. We knew we were capable of making big tackles in the middle but we learned that to win the ruck after the tackle we had to be very aggressive and arrive in numbers. The New Zealand players were attacking the ball on the ground, they did not stay on their feet and they seemed happy to allow their bodies to fall over the ball. Our response had to be decisive – we needed to be more aggressive and dynamic around the space close to the ball. For all that Ben Clarke, Peter Winterbottom and Mike Teague put in some big tackles we did not always win the ball. We had to be much tighter and drive that vital extra half-yard past the ball to create the extra space round the ball to ensure we won it.

This was not Five Nations Championship rugby but British Lions rugby. It added a new dimension to our play which was going to be crucial to our success in the last five weeks of the tour.

Forming up for the scrum. The Maoris are down tight ready to go, while we still have to find our shape ...early days.

The front row ready for another impressive scrummage against Canterbury.

Martin Bayfield comes of age in New Zealand against Canterbury and shows what an outstanding line-jumper he has become.

On the Sunday we flew from Wellington to Christchurch in the South Island for the midweek game against Canterbury. At the first training session for this match I pointed out we would face a slightly different challenge because both Canterbury and Otago had built up a tradition of very aggressive, driving forward play and it was going to be essential to match them. Half the battle was simply to be prepared for a physical war of attrition, because if the players had looked forward to a fluent game of open rugby they would have had a very rude shock. The South Island forwards tend to hunt in very tight groups of three or four, piling into the thick of the action together to try and knock the opposition out of the way. They try, in their own way, to divide and conquer and if they succeeded through their group attacks to splinter our forward effort, they would almost certainly control the loose ball and probably the game.

The Lions needed to have even greater control than usual in the set-piece play so that we didn't allow the Canterbury forwards, who would be quite near the top of any list of good rucking teams, any easy targets or freedom in the open. Solid scrummaging and disciplined, tidy line-outs had to be the order of the day. Our plan was to surprise them by producing our own blend of fierce driving forward play with players combining in numbers to hit the rucks at pace and drive forward to give the backs an extra couple of yards to work with once the ball was delivered.

The Canterbury pack began really well, and winning good possession they were keen to move the ball around. For the first 20 minutes we had to do more than our fair share of defending, and although it was an excellent collective defensive effort on our part I must single out Jeremy Guscott for particular praise. He was absolutely outstanding in everything he did and that included four magnificent tackles which stopped dangerous attacking situations in their tracks. He covered back on another couple of occasions and put in a couple of vital clearing kicks. It was very gratifying to see how one of the world's top attacking players also relished the defensive duties which may not be quite so glamorous but are just as important.

It is never much of a surprise to have to withstand an early barrage of attacking rugby from the New Zealand provincial sides because the match against the Lions is their biggest of the whole season. Once we had weathered the initial storm and blunted their offensive we took the lead. We won tidy line-out possession and near halfway Gibbs linked inside with Ben Clarke, who burst clear in the open. He passed to Jeremy Guscott, who sprinted 30 yards to score. A couple of minutes later Rob Andrew added a penalty, but ten minutes

The irrepressible Ben Clarke playing at open-side wing forward breaks away from the lineout, and always at hand in either attack or defence is Jerry Guscott, ready to take the pass and score a try which covered 45 yards.

before half-time Robert Jones had a clearing kick charged down and Smith scored for Canterbury.

Two very good scrums helped us to increase our lead in the middle of the second half. Our forwards had quickly mastered the art of making that initial hit as the front rows engaged and then immediately beginning the drive almost before the ball was put in. With this momentum in the Lions' favour, the Canterbury forwards were being edged backwards. That provided the perfect opportunity for Rob Andrew to drop a goal from one scrum and Mick Galwey to drive over for a try from another.

In the last 15 minutes Tony Underwood and Rob Andrew each scored a try and all Canterbury could manage in the second half was one penalty. This was an excellent win based on good scrummaging and good line-out ball won by Martin Bayfield, Andy Reed and Ben Clarke. That gave us the advantage in the loose where Ben Clarke and Dean Richards played very well. Once we had taken the sting out of the Canterbury effort, our forwards started to recycle the ball six or seven times in succession, and that was probably the most pleasing aspect of all. One of the highlights for me was when we won a series of rucks and mauls, at least half a dozen, which took play from the halfway line to the Canterbury goal-line. In the UK teams are satisfied to win second- or third-phase possession but we knew in New Zealand we had to recycle the ball five, six, seven or even eight times and we were just beginning to get to grips with this. This had to be the style of the Lions if we were to be successful.

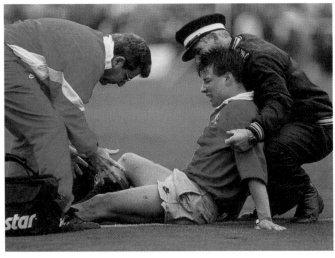

Rob Andrew is injured after scoring his last-minute try and this brings further worries for the management.

We had hoped to pursue the same policy against Otago in Dunedin on the Saturday before the First Test, but after leading 18–8 we allowed Otago back into the match and in a disappointing second half we slumped to our first defeat of the tour. This was obviously worrying because we had selected a strong team which turned out to be just three players short of our Test side.

To be fair to the team, the first half went pretty well. Gavin kicked a penalty in the first minute and even though Cooke scored two tries for Otago after 19 minutes and 38 minutes the rest of the first half, bar one penalty by Bell, belonged to us. Dean Richards and Ieuan Evans scored tries and Gavin added one conversion and a second penalty. What caused concern was the fact that Otago were very keen to open out from good possession from anywhere on the field and we didn't react quickly enough. They scored tries from unlikely situations with bold, adventurous rugby, and for the first time on the tour our defence was found wanting.

Dean Richards' try against Otago completes a very good first-half performance.

The architects of Otago's victory were their half-backs, Stu Forster and Steve Bachop. They both played magnificently and were the main catalysts for almost all five of their tries. Our half-time lead disappeared after 15 minutes of the second half. Leslie and Latta scored tries. Bell converted both and another by Timu soon after Hastings kicked the first of his two second half penalties. It was entirely appropriate that Bachop should have the last word with a drop goal near the end because he was the game's outstanding player.

It was hard to reconcile ourselves to the fact that shortly before half-time we looked to be coasting to victory, yet in the end we suffered the biggest defeat ever inflicted on the Lions by a provincial team. The turning-point

Ieuan Evans' pace again leads to five points, this time against Otago.

OVERLEAF **Consistent possession consistently well used by the Otago half-backs Forster and Bachop forced us on to the defensive.**

came with Cooke's second try just before half-time. Otago had hardly been in our half but had still managed one breakaway try. Then came the second Cooke try. We were on the attack when the ball went loose. Peter Winterbottom and Stuart Barnes went for the ball but an Otago hand got there first and scooped it. Forster and Bachop opened out from their own 22, and with our team all poised to attack as we should have won that loose ball, we were caught on the hop. For once, not enough people were able to get back quickly enough and full marks to Otago for scoring a superb try.

That try seemed to inspire them and they swarmed all over the pitch in the second half. They played tremendously well and it was a great game of rugby, but we should not have been outplayed as we were in that second half. Our biggest problem was not being able to win set-piece possession after half-time. Otago had most of the put-ins to the scrums and, with the Lions in defence regularly having to clear our lines by kicking to touch, they had the majority of the throw-ins to the line-out. We were not the first team to learn how difficult it is to play rugby without the ball. With all this set-piece possession the secret of the Otago team was their ability to play the match in the last 40 minutes two yards our side of the gain-line as a result of their driving forward play. Any New Zealand side which plays the game in that situation is a very dangerous team. It meant we were doing all our tackling from the side and not head-on, and that meant they had continuity going forward all the time. They were able to recycle the ball over and over again and their support play was excellent.

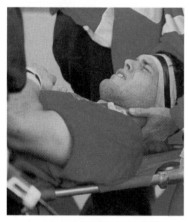

TOP **Martin Bayfield constantly found trouble in the line-out against Otago and this eventually resulted in what we thought at the time was a serious injury.**

We were outplayed in the loose after half-time and we were outplayed at half-back. We can make no excuses because Otago were much the better team in the second half and deserved their triumph. We had a team meeting that evening back in our hotel and everyone knew what had gone wrong. The only consolation was that it was better that we had learned a painful lesson against Otago the week before the Test rather than in the Test itself. We had seven days to get things right.

The first problem we had to overcome was the spate of injuries we suffered in the Otago match and then in the midweek match which followed in Invercargill against Southland. Six players were injured in those two matches, which presented us with all sorts of dilemmas in the week leading up to the First Test.

The most serious looked to be the neck and shoulder double blow which Martin Bayfield sustained near the end of the Otago match. He was upended at a line-out and came crashing down on his neck and back and lay on the ground motionless for several minutes. He was eventually stretchered off and taken to hospital wearing a neck support. He was in a state of shock, and I must admit that at the time it didn't seem as if he had any chance of playing Test match rugby seven days later. It was a fantastic tribute to the team doctor, James Robson, and our physio, Kevin Murphy, that once they had learned nothing was broken they were able to speed up the recovery process to such an extent that Martin was back in training by the middle of the week and was fit for the Test.

Partnering the skipper for a round of golf. He played well: as for me... no comment.

Back to work and looking up to the big boys. When making a point to these fellas I always had to be diplomatic.

An afternoon at the races. Stuart Barnes, the expert, was by far the biggest loser.

Peter Winterbottom, Rory Underwood, Gavin Hastings, Paul Burnell and Ieuan Evans at Invercargill in front of the light aircraft which was about to fly them up to Queenstown for an extra-curricular experience in the mountains with helicopter and paragliders. Thankfully I didn't know about it until afterwards.

The other injuries in Dunedin affected two of the centres. Will Carling strained a muscle at the top of his leg and he limped off the field to be replaced by Scott Hastings. Early in the second half, Scott went into a tackle flat out and received a nasty bang on the face which turned out to be a particularly severe depressed fracture of the cheek. He underwent a four and a half hour operation in Dunedin and, although he stayed with the touring party until the First Test, he then returned to Britain. He was replaced by Vinnie Cunningham, who flew out to New Zealand with Martin Johnson. Martin was invited to join the party when Wade Dooley returned home following the sudden death of his father.

The whole team felt great sympathy for Wade in these very sad circumstances and the New Zealand Council stated that they would invite Wade back if he wished to rejoin the party at a later date. A week after the funeral Wade intimated that he would like to rejoin us for the last two weeks of the tour but it was made clear to the Lions management by the Four Home Unions Committee that once a player had flown home and a replacement had brought the Lions up to full strength, the original player could not play again on the trip. That rule seemed perfectly fair in the case of injury but it struck the Lions as a little unsympathetic in the case of family bereavement.

The Tuesday match was one of the least distinguished of the whole tour and even more frustrating than an unimpressive victory was the sight of both fly-halves leaving the field with bad injuries. Rob Andrew, who had been badly raked in a couple of rucks, broke his nose midway through the second half and left the field bleeding profusely. Ten minutes later Scott Gibbs, who had been our best back and had had another excellent match, fell awkwardly and was carried off with a badly twisted ankle. In injury time Stuart Barnes, who had replaced Rob Andrew, was accidentally trampled on by one of his own team-mates and he was rushed off the field to have 12 stitches inserted into a gaping head wound.

BELOW **An horrific head wound puts Stuart Barnes out of contention for the First Test.**

BOTTOM **A rough and tumble of a game against Southland which proved again that you don't get any easy games in New Zealand.**

Southland, who are in the Second Division, opted to play a spoiling, defensive game and it is often very difficult to look good against a side committed to a damage limitation exercise. Southland had conceded 80 points against Canterbury two weeks previously when, by all accounts, they had lacked real commitment, but we knew they would play until they dropped against the Lions. Taking that into consideration, I felt our win was a satisfactory effort. We raced to a half-time lead of 24–0. Gavin kicked four penalties and converted a penalty try which was awarded when the Southland scrum-half picked the ball out of the Lions scrum five metres from the line with the Lions moving forward. Andy Reed scored a try ten minutes before half-time and Anthony Clement added another ten minutes after the restart. In a less than

Excellent vision under pressure from Tony Underwood leads, two passes later, to Tony Clement scoring between the posts.

dramatic second half Clement dropped a goal for the Lions and Southland scored two tries and two penalties.

Apart from scoring his try Andy Reed had a good match and, with Wade on his way back to England, he did enough to deserve his selection for the Test. There were discussions about the composition of the front row before we settled on Popplewell, Milne and Burnell, but there was no argument about Martin Bayfield at lock or about the back row. Peter Winterbottom was playing really well and I desperately wanted to play both Dean Richards and Ben Clarke. Ben was having a great tour and was chosen for the Test in his third different position in three games – he had played at number eight and open-side flanker before being selected at blind side for the Test.

In Australia and Asia we're all over the place.

We've been flying long-haul for longer than any other airline. It's our experience which makes your experience of flying with us so pleasurable. We fly the very latest 747-400's from London and Manchester to over 30 destinations in Australia and Asia. More than any other airline. More often. For details of our fares and schedules to Asia or Australia, call 0345 747 767, or contact your travel agent.

QANTAS

TANTALISINGLY CLOSE
THE FIRST TEST MATCH

As you can see from my notes on the following page, the planning for a Test match begins on the Sunday six days before. I watched and edited videos of the Lions matches to show, in 20 minutes of highlights, a list of key areas in which we had performed well and badly in previous games. I froze the edited film to show where things had worked well and to explain what had been going wrong, why it had been going wrong and how to improve it. I did all the editing myself, not only of the Lions matches but usually also videos of our next opponents so that I was able to talk about and illustrate their strengths and weaknesses and could isolate a lot of action which might help individual players to improve their game.

For each training session I planned a whole series of special routines, all with a view to the next big match. On the Monday prior to the Test I would work with the team for the Tuesday match but also start working on specific exercises for the probable Test combinations for the Saturday. By the Wednesday, the intensity of the build-up to the Test was being felt. We worked on a series of line-out variations. We did some really competitive scrummaging and slotted in an extra secret scrummaging session on the Wednesday evening. We made sure we were spot on in practice and then worked with opposition. The backs ran at speed at the correct angles and concentrated on good, quick, accurate passing. They worked three against two and four against three, knowing they might only get one chance or half-chance in the Test and that it could be the winning or the losing of the match. The backs concentrated on their angles of running the depth of the line, the trajectory and the speed of the pass and on a handful of moves we had added to our repertoire with code names like World Cup and World Class.

The training at the closed private sessions on the Wednesday and the Thursday involved a whole range of line-out variations including two-man, three-man and four-man line-outs with Martin Bayfield jumping at the front, in the middle and at the back, on both our throw and their throw. We practised with group formations at the line-out, trying one group of four followed by a little gap and another group of three. We were determined not to be too predictable on our ball.

We practised back-row moves in attack and tried to perfect our whole defensive organisation at the set pieces and in the loose play. Friday was to be a light session with the emphasis on speed in everything we did. We had team meetings each evening and went over in detail everything we had to achieve on the Saturday. I spelled out all the individual responsibilities of each of the 15 players and I emphasised all the collective responsibilities as well. Nothing was left to chance.

For example, we knew it would be difficult to win the All Blacks' line-out ball because just as scrum-halves in New Zealand are, apparently, all allowed to put the ball in squint at the scrums, making the art of hooking almost obsolete, so the hooker takes half a pace towards his side at the line-out before throwing in dead straight. By dead straight I mean at exactly 90 degrees to the touchline,

Planning ahead for the Test Match.

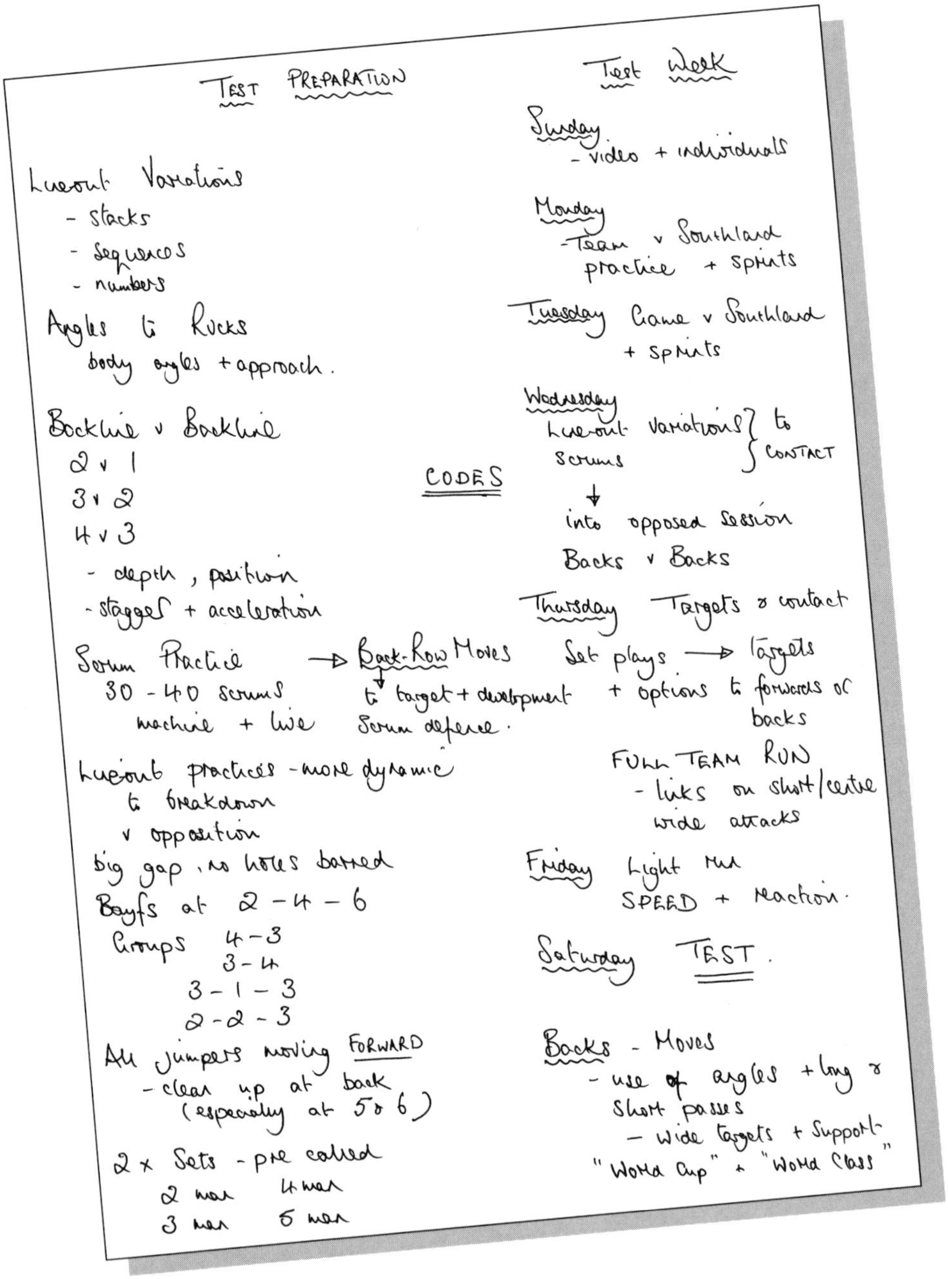

TEST PREPARATION

Lineout Variations
- stacks
- sequences
- numbers

Angles to Rucks
body angles + approach.

Backline v Backline
2 v 1
3 v 2
4 v 3
- depth, position
- stagger + acceleration

Scrum Practice → Back-Row Moves
30 - 40 scrums   to target + development
machine + live   Scrum defence.

CODES

Lineout practices - more dynamic
to breakdown
v opposition
big gap, no holes barred
Boyfs at 2 - 4 - 6
Groups   4 - 3
         3 - 4
       3 - 1 - 3
       2 - 2 - 3
All jumpers moving FORWARD
- clean up at back
(especially at 5 or 6)
2 x Sets - pre called
2 man   4 man
3 man   5 man

TEST WEEK

Sunday
- video + individuals

Monday
- Team v Southland
practice + sprints

Tuesday Game v Southland
+ sprints

Wednesday
Lineout variations } to
Scrums   } CONTACT
↓
into opposed session
Backs v Backs

Thursday   Targets + contact
Set plays → Targets
+ options to forwards or
backs

FULL TEAM RUN
- links on short/centre
wide attacks

Friday   Light run
SPEED + reaction.

Saturday   TEST.

Backs - Moves
- use of angles + long or
short passes
- wide targets + support
"World Cup" + "World Class"

but because he is standing half a pace nearer his players than ours, the ball is not thrown in to the middle of the line-out. That gives his jumpers an advantage, so I tried to reduce the number of times we kicked the ball to touch. Instead, even in defensive situations, I planned for our half-backs to kick high into that narrow area between the touchline and the five-yard line, about 20 or 25 yards over our forwards. It was then vital that our first-up players arrived at the same time as the ball and either rucked it back or forced the catcher into touch to give us the throw to the line-out.

Another example was in loose play, where we spent a great deal of time creating space round the ball in open play. So if Jeremy Guscott took a crash ball in the centre, made a few valuable yards and then went to ground, I needed our first five support players to react immediately and dynamically to that particular situation, just like the great All Black sides do. The first two, be they backs or forwards, would not necessarily go for the ball unless it could be quickly won and recycled. They would thunder into any advancing opponents in what I describe as a dynamic ruck situation to stop them impeding our next support players' efforts to secure the ball on the ground. In a low driving position, the rest of the forwards, legs pumping, would spreadeagle the opposition and produce good loose ball for the Lions. Then the ball could be picked up, a new target area selected and the whole process repeated. The idea was to recycle the ball in this way half a dozen times or more, varying the target areas all the time and, of course, always being prepared to spin the ball along the threequarter line if there was an overlap begging. This dynamic rucking was equally effective in defensive situations when the All Blacks had the ball and went to ground. Our first priority was to create the space around the ball to stop them winning it or even win it ourselves.

I mentioned that the players nearest the ball had to react rapidly whether they happened to be backs or forwards. Against Auckland, for example, the ball-carrier, Nick Popplewell, set up a ruck and the first there to drive into the opposition and secure the space round the ball was Rob Andrew. Instantly he drove forward just like a forward would be expected to do, across Popplewell into the Auckland players. We won the ruck and the ball sped to Scott Gibbs, along the line via Gavin Hastings to Ieuan Evans, who scored. After the match people asked me where Rob Andrew had been in that move, and the answer was helping to win the ruck.

The preparation for the Test went really well and the Lions were very confident. Conditions were good at Lancaster Park in Christchurch and everyone sensed that this really was the biggest match of the tour thus far by a very long way.

An international match has a certain tension and buzz that no other game of rugby has, and for a British player, no matter how important an England-Wales game or a Calcutta Cup match may be, nothing quite compares with a Test between the British Lions and the New Zealand All Blacks. This is the ultimate confrontation – the supreme challenge that the game has to offer.

Irrespective of how well prepared or even how confident both teams were, the first quarter of the match was bound to produce a sprinkling of tentative rugby. In fact, for much of the first half, nerves got the better of both teams and there were a lot of mistakes made, especially unforced errors. This was particularly bad news for the Lions, because we played with the wind in the first half and really needed to settle in quickly and take full advantage of the elements to build up a lead. But what was much worse, we found ourselves five points down in the opening two minutes of the match to a very controversial try.

The sequence of events which led to the try has been well chronicled. Fox launched a high kick to the corner with deadly accuracy which Ieuan Evans caught. Frank Bunce arrived a split second later and he wrapped his hands round the ball as well. At that point both players, still holding the ball between them, crashed down over the goal-line. Ieuan never relinquished his grip on the ball and yet the referee, from several yards off the pace, awarded the try.

All I can say is that if the whole situation had been reversed and the Lions had been attacking I would have been delighted if we had been awarded a try, but I would not have expected it. To most people at the game and to the millions of armchair critics watching on television there seemed to have been an element of doubt and, to the best of my knowledge, if the referee has any doubt, he should award a five-metre scrum.

I have spoken to a few famous international referees since the Christchurch Test and they all are in agreement on two counts. First, it was significant that Ieuan caught the ball first and kept his grip on it from that moment until the try was actually awarded. He had first touch of the ball, squatter's rights, as it were, and never, at any stage, did he let go of the ball. That in itself should have been enough to persuade the referee not to award a try – he surely could not have been certain Bunce had scored. Had Bunce caught the ball before Ieuan it could be argued differently, but he did not. Secondly, if there was a real element of doubt, which there surely was, the referee was duty bound to give a scrum and not a try.

It would have been unwelcome at any stage of the Test, but to concede a try right at the very beginning was unquestionably a bitter blow. It was very encouraging that the Lions fought their way back into contention and managed to take the lead midway through the half with two penalties by Gavin.

Beginning to shape up with body positions to match New Zealand.

Before half-time Fox kicked two penalties for the All Blacks and Gavin kicked a third for the Lions to leave the All Blacks leading 11-9. It is not in my nature to spend my time moaning and criticising referees, even if the most talked-about of our penalties in the first half definitely had the word 'try' stamped all over it.

A jerky threequarter line movement which we started in our own half eventually set free Jeremy Guscott on the left flank. He glided down the touchline with only the full-back, John Timu, to beat. On his inside, in support, he could see and hear Will Carling, and just as he prepared to give the scoring pass to Will, Michael Jones yanked Will by the jersey. Jerry instantly had to go it alone and had Will not been there in the first place he would have had plenty of time to kick past Timu and chase the ball to the line. Unfortunately, with Will hors de combat, he had to hurriedly chip over Timu and the ball bounced

off Timu into touch. The referee penalised Jones for tackling Will Carling without the ball and Gavin kicked the penalty for three points, but I think everyone at the match would agree that had Michael Jones not illegally taken out Carling, then Guscott would have passed and Carling would almost certainly have scored between the posts and given us seven points.

It really was wretched luck. Afterwards the referee, Brian Kinsey, was quoted as saying that he briefly considered awarding a penalty try, but I have no doubt he made the right decision because the incident was a long way from the New Zealand line.

In the second half the Lions played some of their best rugby of the tour. We were doing well in the set pieces and having much the better of the argument in the loose. Peter Winterbottom, Dean Richards and Ben Clarke were in superlative form and they were inspirational throughout the second half as the Lions, by grit and ruthless determination, clawed their way back into the match playing into the wind. Martin Bayfield did remarkably well – after just two seasons of international rugby, here he was in the real pressure cooker atmosphere of an All Black Test with all the rough and tumble and very physical intensity of the line-out, not yielding an inch and winning his fair share of quality possession. It was a tremendous effort and he also contributed well in the open.

The scrummage was the best it had been in the first seven matches and I think we surprised the All Blacks with our solidity and stability as they had expected to be dominant in this phase of play. Nonetheless, we were slightly less than comfortable on our own ball, being just rocked back a fraction and

LEFT It takes both Ieuan Evans and Ben Clarke to stop Inga Tuigamala. He was to be a handful in all three Tests.

Gavin Hastings lines up one of his six penalty kicks which saw the Lions overhaul the All Blacks' early lead.

wheeled a fraction. It was not serious by any means, but there was still a little room for improvement.

Apart from that 'try' at the start, it was very heartening that the All Blacks never really threatened to score. Our defence was better than their attack and only Tuigamala posed any problems. As we knew beforehand, their main scoring weapon was Grant Fox. He kicked another two penalties in the first

quarter of an hour of the second half but so did Gavin Hastings, which left New Zealand two points ahead with 25 minutes remaining. We played some excellent controlled rugby and gradually we were gaining the initiative. With just ten minutes to go the All Blacks were penalised at a ruck about 40 yards out and nearer the touchline than midfield. Not only had Gavin played magnificently at full-back throughout the tour, he had also kicked so well at goal that the punters had elevated him to very near the Grant Fox pedestal. If ever there was a pressure kick, this was it; into the wind from a tricky angle with the fate of the First Test hanging in the balance. He struck it perfectly and it soared between the posts. The Lions took the lead 18-17. Suddenly, the game was there for the winning.

We had continued to play with control from the restart and the seconds were ticking away. With just one minute left, the referee landed the real killer blow. He awarded an amazingly controversial penalty against the Lions in midfield near our ten-metre line. Dean Richards had tackled Frank Bunce and, quite legitimately, turned him towards our side. The ball was released and it had been retrieved by Dewi Morris when Brian Kinsey blew his whistle and penalised us. It appeared an outrageous decision at the time and one that I was simply at a loss to explain, and having watched it again a hundred times on the video I am still unable to explain satisfactorily why we were penalised. Fox kicked the goal and we found ourselves one Test down in a three-Test series.

I know that into every life a little rain must fall but we seemed to suffer an unfair deluge on a clear, dry day in Christchurch. We held no review of the Test that Saturday evening. The team sat in silence in the changing room, stunned by the events of the opening two minutes and the last two minutes of the match. The Lions were heroic in defeat but they were only too well aware that you don't win gold medals for coming second.

We were bitterly disappointed at losing a game we could and should have won. But at the same time there was a genuine feeling of optimism and confidence in our camp. We knew we were as good, and quite possibly better than the All Blacks, and there was every reason to believe we would be good enough to win the Second Test and square the series. As far as we were concerned the Test series was far from over – it was only just beginning.

Grant Fox follows the flight of his last-minute penalty.

A TOUGH TWO WEEKS

On the Sunday we flew from Christchurch to New Plymouth to begin the rehabilitation programme against Taranaki.

The few days we spent in Taranaki were greatly appreciated by the party because there was a really warm provincial feel about the place. For the locals it was their biggest day of the year and they were determined to celebrate in style. They laid on a wonderful parade through the town with decorated floats and then a huge crowd of 25,000 packed Rugby Park for the match. It was nice to see hundreds of schoolkids thronging the pitch and they clearly loved the whole occasion, not just because they got off school for the afternoon but because they experienced a day they would always remember.

With two bandits on the first green at New Plymouth.

We won by 49 points to 25 in a highly entertaining game which produced almost a point per minute and ten tries, seven scored by the Lions. The midweek team displayed the same attitude and commitment as the Saturday side in this match – even though they were not to repeat it the following week in Napier – and I was very pleased with the performances of Jason Leonard at tight-head prop, Martin Johnson at lock and Scott Gibbs in the centre. I was also delighted that scrum-half Andy Nicol, who had flown in from Scotland's tour of Western Samoa as a temporary replacement because

Rucking and driving practice at New Plymouth. Our body positions are getting much better. So is the use of our hands and feet for binding.

Martin Johnson makes an impressive debut against Taranaki.

Robert Jones was suffering from tonsillitis, got on for the last seven minutes. He played his heart out in that short time and is now a British Lion.

To score 49 points against any First Division side in New Zealand is a pretty good achievement and I was very pleased with this result even though we had a few lapses of concentration which allowed Taranaki to score three tries. Our forwards dominated the set pieces and we were a couple of yards faster in the open, which provided the perfect platform for the backs to cut loose. Having said that, it took us the best part of half an hour to subdue a very lively Taranaki side which actually led 13-6 ten minutes before half-time. Former All Black full-back Kieran Crowley kicked two penalties and converted a try by their lock forward, Bernie O'Sullivan.

Stuart Barnes kicked two penalties for the Lions and then, in a powerful surge just before half-time, he converted two tries scored by Damian Cronin and Mike Teague. In the second half the backs made good use of good possession and ran in five more tries against two for Taranaki. Vinnie Cunningham scored two and Robert Jones, Richard Wallace and Scott Gibbs got one each.

That final try capped another excellent performance by Gibbs, who had performed well in every single match he had played on the tour, and this latest effort, coupled with the fact that Will Carling was not scaling the heights as he had done in the Five Nations Championship during the 1990s, earned Gibbs a deserved chance in the Saturday side. His selection for the Auckland match was not, in any way, a major criticism of Carling because he was tackling and defending as well as ever and was playing very steady rugby. But he admitted himself that the spark which has made him one of the top four centres in world rugby in the past three years was missing. He had had to overcome some minor niggling injuries on the tour – two different leg aggravations and then a damaged shoulder – and the fact is things just did not run his way.

The other changes for the Auckland match from the First Test side saw Jason Leonard brought in at tight-head prop, Brian Moore at hooker and Martin Johnson at lock. Unfortunately, we had to make two changes before the match because Leonard had a badly bruised leg and a slight shoulder injury and Dean Richards withdrew with a pulled calf muscle. The game against Auckland was generally regarded as the unofficial Fourth Test and we certainly treated it as the most important game of the tour outside the actual Tests. If

Andy Nicol during six splendid minutes in a Lions jersey.

I put it into context, we were taking on the best non-international rugby side in the world. Apart from the fact that they contained ten All Blacks, they had not lost a match against a touring team since 1981 and they were the current holders of the Ranfurly Shield. That trophy is the most prized possession in provincial rugby and the holders have to accept a number of one-off challenges from other provincial sides each year. Auckland, would you believe, had defended the Shield successfully in 59 challenges in the past decade in a run of unprecedented success.

This record meant there was more than a hint of jealousy among the other provinces and several supporters from outside Auckland genuinely hoped we would win. We made an inauspicious start. We were penalised in the opening minute and Grant Fox kicked the goal. A few minutes later, Gavin Hastings levelled the scores with a penalty and then, after 24 minutes, gave the Lions the

lead with a conversion after the referee, David Bishop, perhaps a shade generously, awarded us a penalty try when Auckland collapsed a maul near their line.

Two minutes later, as Auckland swept downfield on the attack and used the blind side, Rory Underwood slipped as he tried to turn round and as

Ieuan Evans leaves behind a trail of defenders to score an outstanding try against Auckland.

he lay on the ground near our line, John Kirwan chased a kick ahead to score Auckland's only try of the match. In the last ten minutes of the half, the Lions increased their lead with a brilliant try. Popplewell set up a ruck in midfield, the ball flashed along the threequarter line to Ieuan Evans, who danced inside

The backs attack from different angles against Auckland. Jerry has four options here depending on how he reads the defence.

RIGHT **Grant Fox brings Lee Stensness into the game, and a good performance from the youngster leads to an All Black jersey.**

the wing and past the cover to score in the corner. With Fox and Andrew each kicking a penalty we led 18-11 at half-time after playing our best 40 minutes of rugby up to that point.

We played with tremendous control up front to have the better of the line-outs and we held our own in the scrums. Once again, I thought we were outstanding in the loose, with Peter Winterbottom and Ben Clarke quite immense and Mike Teague getting through a power of work in the hard, physical, close-quarter exchanges. Martin Bayfield had another splendid match and I made him our man of the match when I was asked to make this decision by the Auckland Supporters Club. They chose Scott Gibbs, which was not at all surprising. The half-backs, Dewi Morris and Rob Andrew, were playing with great authority and taking all the right options, and the backs scarcely made a mistake in the entire half.

The first hiccup occurred in our last attack before half-time when Gavin Hastings burst into the line to make a real dent in the Auckland midfield defence but slightly pulled a hamstring in the process. He was replaced at full-back by Will Carling, which gave our back division an uneven feel. Our pack lost overall control in the second half and we made a few errors under pressure.

Our defensive organisation and commitment remained excellent and we never threatened to concede another try, but our attacking opportunities were limited. Auckland had the majority of throws to the line-out, which restricted our options. We had one great chance to score a try early in the second half, which I am certain would have clinched the match. Ben Clarke led a thundering forward drive and was stopped two feet from the line. He fell to the ground and in a second movement placed the ball over the line. The Lions supporters cheered for a try but the referee quite rightly penalised Clarke for playing the ball after he had been tackled. Had he simply left the ball on the ground two feet short, our forwards driving through may well have scored, but it was not to be and that was the last try-scoring chance for either side.

The story of the rest of the match was a rather familiar one – a couple of moments of indiscipline and a couple of strange refereeing decisions presented Fox with four penalty kicks at goal. He put them all over for a final tally in the match of six out of six. It was all very frustrating as we had come desperately close to producing a top-class performance.

However, for three Saturdays in a row, against Otago, New Zealand and Auckland, we had played really well for 40 minutes and not so well for the other 40. If only we could have produced our effort for the whole 80 minutes we would have won all three of those matches. If only. But, as the Lions team manager, Geoff Cooke, said afterwards, the two most utterly useless words in the English language are 'if only...'

Martin Johnson, once again in the thick of things against Auckland.

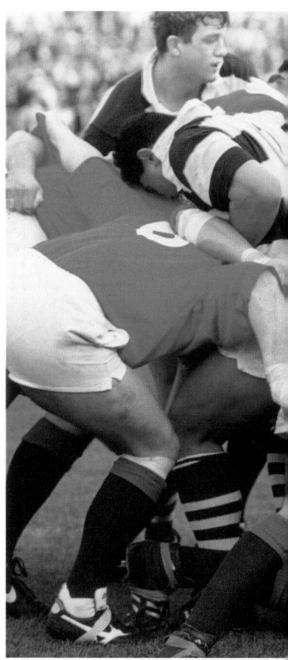

Nonetheless, we knew then that if we could play for the whole 80 minutes in Wellington the following Saturday the way we had played in the first half against Auckland we would win the Second Test. If we didn't, we wouldn't. It was all that simple.

At least, even in defeat, there had been plenty of positive lessons to come out of the Auckland game. Martin Johnson showed himself to be up to Test match rugby at lock and so did Scott Gibbs in the centre. They were both pencilled in for the Second Test. The half-backs, Andrew and Morris, had established their status and Brian Moore, with a fiery, competitive display, had edged marginally ahead of Kenny Milne at hooker. We were close to knowing our best Test line-up judged on current form as the tour had developed and evolved, but we still needed to see Leonard at tight-head prop. Paul Burnell had been very reliable and steady and had certainly not let the Lions down, but he had not been as active in the open as he had always been for Scotland and we felt Jason Leonard might just lock the scrum on the right-hand side a fraction better and be a shade more dynamic in the open. Fully recovered from his minor leg and shoulder problems, he was picked at tight head for the match against Hawke's Bay in Napier.

This match was a last chance for the 15 midweek dirt-trackers to stake a claim in the Test side because it had to be assumed that if we did win the Second Test we would be very likely to keep the same side for the final Test. Bearing that in mind there should have been every incentive for the players to make a supreme effort against Hawke's Bay. For some inexplicable reason it

RIGHT One of the few bright spots in the Hawke's Bay game was the very positive running performance of Will Carling.

just didn't happen. Perhaps it was because the players felt that, in reality, the Test side was more or less finalised. In fact it wasn't, and we were still interested in the efforts of several players. Admittedly, each of these players would have needed to have had an outstanding game to make the Test side, but that in itself gave me every reason to anticipate half a dozen major individual performances.

Nothing could have been further from the truth. On every tour of 13 matches there has to be one game which stands out as far and away the worst 80 minutes of the whole tour. In 1993, it was our defeat by Hawke's Bay. In Napier we hit rock bottom. There was the unmistakable sound of the scraping of the bottom of the barrel. We could sink no lower. I'm afraid it was just one of those dismal displays which defies description. Yet, oddly enough, the first half went reasonably well.

Carling dropped a goal early on, Richard Webster scored a try midway through the half and Stuart Barnes

kicked three penalties. Hawke's Bay captain Norm Hewitt replied with a try but the Lions had much the better of the first half and deserved their lead of 17-5. One thing I stressed to the Lions throughout the tour was that no new Zealand side will ever give up and that it was essential to play flat out right to the final whistle. That did not happen in Napier and we paid the penalty. We fell apart in the second half and most of the blame lay with the pack. One or two guys like Will Carling and Mike Teague played flat out

The Hawke's Bay hooker Stormin' Norm Hewitt, who had such an outstanding game against the Lions.

and Stuart Barnes and Richard Webster also performed well, but for the majority it was a game they would all be very happy to forget.

Some critics said the second half was the worst 40 minutes of rugby ever played by a British Lions side. I don't know about that, but it was certainly one of the most inept and disappointing efforts by an international side that I can recall. Of all the things which went wrong during our eight weeks in New Zealand, I think the last 40 minutes in Napier would be very near the top of the list. It was simply awful. Hawke's Bay scored two more tries, three penalties and a drop goal in a one-sided second half. They showed more commitment and urgency and deserved their win.

We had very little consolation from our mediocre performance, but even though we had suffered a bad psychological blow and it definitely didn't do our morale any good, it bore very little relevance to Saturday's Test. In Wellington 14 different players plus Jason Leonard would represent the Lions and we would be into a whole new ball game. The stakes would be raised, but then so would our performance.

Stop off en route, en us.

AUSTRALIA

HONG KONG
BALI
BANGKOK
SINGAPORE
KUALA LUMPUR
JAKARTA

We'll show you the sights few visitors to Australia ever see.

Hop off to Australia with us, and you can break your journey in Asia free. With 6 exotic locations to choose from, it's quite a departure.

That's hardly surprising. We're high fliers when it comes to long haul flights. We've a fleet of the latest 747's leaving Heathrow and Manchester daily. Flying you to your destination in award-winning comfort.

For more information about our services to Australia call Qantas on 0345 747767, or contact your travel agent.

We'll add the Far East to your itinerary. But not your fare.

RECORD PERFORMANCE
THE SECOND TEST MATCH

We had quite an involved selection meeting on the Tuesday night before finalising the team for the Second Test. The one calculated risk we all agreed to take was the selection of Jason Leonard at tight-head prop. He had played there at school but had played all his senior rugby on the loose head. The person most directly under pressure at the set scrum, if Jason was in trouble, would be the hooker, and we had opted for Brian Moore to take over this role from Kenny Milne. We discussed the props with Brian and he said he was perfectly happy to have Leonard on the tight-head.

To try to improve our line-out play we decided to pick Martin Johnson at lock in place of Andy Reed and that gave us four genuine jumpers in Bayfield, Johnson, Clarke and Richards. I felt the line-out was going to be an absolutely crucial area in the Test and I wanted the greatest amount of ammunition I could possibly muster.

The only change in the back division was the inclusion of Scott Gibbs in the centre in place of Will Carling. This was an extremely difficult decision, although it was also a unanimous one, because we were losing an awful lot of experience in dropping Will and he had shown real signs of a return to form with a first-class game against Hawke's Bay. However, on balance, it was agreed that Scott Gibbs had shown consistently outstanding form over a five-week period and he deserved a crack at the All Blacks.

We decided not to announce the team on the Wednesday because we had two major injury worries. Dean Richards was making good progress with his pulled calf muscle, but Gavin Hastings was far from confident that he would recover from his hamstring injury in time to play. We had a private training session in Napier on the Wednesday in which the backs and forwards split up for most of the time to concentrate on their own unit skills. The backs did a lot of running and passing under pressure making sure that by their angles of running and their sheer pace they could turn every situation of two players against one, three against two and four against three into an overlap. The emphasis was on acceleration and I worked hard on achieving the most lethal attacks by exploiting a staggered start so that the whole threequarter line did not sprint up to the gain-line in formation all at the same time but in a slightly varied line-up so that at the right moment the player about to receive the ball could inject real pace into the movement by instant acceleration. All the back play was very sharp at this session and I was delighted.

The forwards initially worked really hard on the set pieces with the pack scrummaging against live opposition, not against a machine, between 30 and 35 times. At the very end of the Thursday session they had another 20 to 25

The ultimate challenge in New Zealand. Inga Tuigamala personifies the Haka.

scrums and this grinding, rather unglamorous grafting paid real dividends in Wellington.

On the Wednesday the pack also practised a lot of line-out variations against live opposition with the ball being thrown to every jumper in a prolonged specialist line-out practice. On our own throw we had to be alert and aware to tidy up immediately any tapped or palmed possession. In the Test, Popplewell, Leonard and Winterbottom excelled at protecting and securing ball which we touched first. They made untidy ball into tidy ball. We practised two-man, three-man and four-man line-outs and, with live opposition, we also tried to spoil on their throw-in. We changed all our line-out codes for the Second Test just in case the All Blacks had worked them out in the First Test. There was a tremendous sense of urgency to this whole practice session and it went very well indeed.

We practised a handful of back-row moves and we also targeted back-row defence with live opposition; we practised kick-offs for and against and also

Nick Popplewell bursting away from a line-out yet again, and showing the dynamic rugby which was so much a part of his play.

worked on a few moves from free kicks. Nothing, but nothing, was left to chance. The backs worked really intensely on their defensive organisation and after about an hour and a half of furious physical training, the backs and forwards came together for 15 or 20 minutes of semi-opposed rugby.

That afternoon back at the hotel I called for a special meeting of eight of the senior players to come to my room to discuss in detail our plans for the Test. The backs were represented by Gavin Hastings, Rob Andrew, Jeremy Guscott and Ieuan Evans; the forwards by Dean Richards, Peter Winterbottom, Brian Moore and Nick Popplewell. We discussed at length how we were going to play the game and what role each and every one of the 15 would have both individually and collectively. We spent half an hour discussing exactly what we had to achieve in the Test and also how we would stop the All Blacks. We worked out how we would dominate the line-out, surprise them in the scrums and outplay them in the loose. We talked about tackling and how important it was for all 15 of the team to each be prepared to put in as many tackles as it required to snuff out the opposition. This was one of our great strengths – in the first two Tests all New Zealand could manage in the way of tries was to follow up two high kicks from Grant Fox and hope for a couple of mistakes from the Lions. Scarcely brilliant, positive rugby.

The Thursday session, it was agreed with these senior players, would be a quite different session from all the others we had had on the tour. We decided to spend the best part of two hours without any opposition working on specific set-piece rugby. We practised line-outs in a load of different positions on the field of play from one goal-line to the other. I said, right, if we win a line-out here, 30 metres from the All Blacks line, what will we do? We made our choice and then did it. We had a range of scrums up and down the whole length of the field so everyone knew what we would try to do if we were in midfield or 20 metres from the left-hand touchline or ten metres from the right-hand touchline. We repeated this with rucks and mauls all over the field. It got everyone thinking along the same lines, on precisely the same wavelength. It was a good way to break up the normal routine and yet still get every single one of the players to start focusing their whole attention on the match on Saturday afternoon at Athletic Park in Wellington.

It was not so much a physical session as a cerebral session. The "think tank" dominated everything. It was all stop-start with animated discussion on what we would do in this particular situation and why we do it and how we do it. The whole two hours was about attacking play and what we would do with the ball in each and every situation. I was by this stage of the tour satisfied with our defence so the entire emphasis on the Thursday was on offensive play.

On the Thursday evening we had a team meeting with a blackboard lesson during which we went over everything we had covered at training that morning. This underlined and consolidated our whole tactical approach and helped each player to focus on the Test. We had added a couple of extra moves for the backs and we went over these in detail for the benefit of not just the threequarters but the forwards as well.

I was delighted with the way Thursday went and on Friday morning I put the team through only the lightest of light training. They worked at real pace for ten minutes without a single mistake and I called a halt. We were ready for the All Blacks. Not a pass was dropped, every pass was fast and accurate, and the support play was excellent, as was the rucking and mauling against the contact pads which were held by some of the midweek dirt-trackers. Every player knew that on Saturday we would have to be good enough and fast enough and strong enough to recycle the ball in the loose – over and over and over again. Fortunately, we were.

However, as the forwards went off to do some scrummaging, I was left with Gavin Hastings to make the most important decision of the tour. Was he fit to play? He felt the hamstring was still tight and even though he completed the sharp ten-minute session he reckoned he should not play because it still wasn't right. He thought it would probably go early on and that he would let the team down if he had to leave the field after five minutes. I was desperate for him to play but he was totally unconvinced. I left him with the team manager, Geoff Cooke, and went off to have a word with Jeremy Guscott and Rob Andrew.

They both agreed with me 100 per cent that he should start the game, come what may, because he had become such an inspirational leader that it would give the team a huge boost to have him as the focal point for our final 24-hour build-up. He was such an influential player, oozing confidence, that he inspired everyone around him. Reassured by Rob and Jeremy and exhorted by me, he agreed to give it a go. That was the first turning-point of the match. It had been touch and go all week and on Friday Gavin was far from convinced he would survive 80 fast, furious and frenetic minutes of a Test match. However,

RIGHT **Scott Gibbs breaks through the New Zealand defence to put them on the back foot.**

BELOW RIGHT **Tight support in numbers for every Lion who was tackled with the ball.**

OVERLEAF **Down tight and ready for action. Our scrum is in very good shape.**

once the decision was made at 11 o'clock on Friday morning, he became utterly positive and immediately told the throng of journalists that everything was perfect and he was raring to go. The team meeting that evening lasted well over an hour. With the help of a blackboard, we went over every single detail of the match one final time to reinforce all the hours of talk and practice we had had that week. I did most of the talking but Rob Andrew, Gavin Hastings, Brian Moore and Dean Richards all made valuable contributions. On Saturday morning we had a last briefing in our team room at the hotel before lunch. The tension was beginning to get to me. When I went into the dining room, I realised there was no way I could face any food. That had never happened to me before. I slipped back to my room where I had asked for all the team jerseys to be delivered. After lunch, each player came to my room to collect his jersey and I had a last chance to offer a final few words of encouragement and advice. I went over just one or two of the most important points as they affected each player individually. As we boarded the coach to drive to the ground I felt our preparation had been as painstakingly thorough as it could possibly have been.

Once the team reaches the changing rooms my role is finished and the captain takes over. But after walking from one end of the pitch to the other, it

was patently clear that there was going to be a big advantage playing with the wind. The team playing against it would also be facing an incredibly bright sun which would make following the flight of a high kick extremely difficult. Gavin and I decided that if we won the toss we would play the first half into the wind.

Now that may seem a strange decision, but we had played with the elements in our favour in the first half of the First Test and it had taken both sides most of that time to settle down after a nervous, tentative start and we had therefore been unable to take full advantage of our 40 minutes with the wind. I also felt very strongly that after our intense thorough build-up to the Second Test nothing would focus our minds more than playing into the wind and the sun in the first-half. From the kick-off every player would have to play to his absolute maximum potential to contain the All Blacks and they would all know that one lapse of concentration playing against the elements could prove very expensive. Playing against the wind would surely concentrate everyone's minds wonderfully. We

Another line-out win for Martin Bayfield, the crucial area in which we did so well in the Second Test.

won the toss and gave New Zealand first use of the wind and the sun.

For the whole of the first half, bar one mistake, the Lions played fantastic rugby and virtually everything we had practised for the previous six weeks and especially the previous three days we executed to very near perfection. We not only won the line-outs 14 to 7 but the quality of our possession was much better. We had learned from the defeats of the previous three Saturdays and we worked

hard at getting the throw-in to the line-out. Instead of kicking to touch we kicked, as we had practised, down the touchline but keeping the ball in play. Morris and Andrew produced a series of precision kicks right through the match. We had the better of the scrummage with Leonard, Moore and Johnson contributing greatly and one of the turning-points of the match came at a scrum five near our line in the second half when the All Blacks went for a push-over try. Here all the unglamorous scrummaging practice we had done in training really paid off. Not only did we hold them, but we did it so comfortably that we actually pushed them back, and for most of that time Dean Richards was even able to have his head out of the scrum ready to react if they resorted to a back-row move. With the attempted push-over comfortably thwarted, the All Blacks had to try their back-row move on the retreat and the threat was easily contained.

That was one of five major turning-points which decided the outcome of this Test in our favour. The first was when the team knew Gavin would play. The third came with Rob Andrew's superb left-footed drop goal just before half-time. That meant we turned round to play with the elements in the second half with a lead of two points, which left us almost impregnable. The second half provided two further focal points which turned the match even more in favour of the Lions. First, there was the try by Rory Underwood, which was the culmination of a combined flash of genius from Guscott and Underwood. This was the sort of brilliance the Lions backs had always threatened to produce and the All Blacks, in the same circumstances, had not. Secondly, for all our innumerable great tackles, there was one which must have destroyed All Black confidence. John Kirwan, their record try-scorer, accelerated towards the Lions on a major run only to find Ben Clarke in his path. Clarke not only stopped Kirwan stone dead in his tracks, he immediately frog-marched him backwards several yards. Added together, these individual turning-points combined to leave the All Blacks all at sea. It was game, set and match.

The only blemish in the first half came when Grant Fox put up a high kick from our 22 and Gavin Hastings, standing on his goal-line, had to look directly into the sun to follow it. He was in the perfect position but the ball popped out of his arms as he turned towards the touchline away from the glare of the sun and even though Scott Gibbs, Rory Underwood and Dean Richards had all raced back and were right there, Eroni Clarke got the bounce of the ball and scored. Fox converted and after 13 minutes the Lions were trailing by 7–0.

It says a great deal for the Lions that New Zealand never scored again. One major reason for this was our remarkable discipline. Throughout that entire 40-minute period playing into the wind we did not give away one single kickable penalty to Grant Fox. It had been over five years since Fox had failed

LEFT **Rob Andrew puts in another kick with pinpoint accuracy to send the All Blacks back again.**

BELOW LEFT **After three very good decisions Rory Underwood scores my favourite try of the tour.**

All Blacks on the ground, the Lions players on their feet, well focused and intent on winning the Test match.

to kick a penalty in an international. In fact, the last time was against Wales in 1988 when New Zealand won 52-3. For all their pressure, we showed immense control and discipline and made sure we were not penalised. Not so the All Blacks. They gave Gavin Hastings four kicks at goal in the first half, almost all of them from the same spot 30 metres out on the right. The first two attempts missed narrowly, one hitting an upright, but the next two soared over in the ten minutes before half-time. We would have been quite satisfied to turn round 7 – 6 down before exploiting our second-half advantage. I made my way down from the stand to ask the team doctor James Robson, to tell the players at half-time that they dare not relax just because we would have the wind in the second half;

You never beat the All Blacks – you only score more points. Jamie Joseph shows their determination to try to get back at us during the Second Test.

OVERLEAF **The Gulliver's travellers, part of a huge contingent of British supporters.**

that they must redouble their efforts, focus and concentrate even harder and make sure they played the game in the All Blacks' half of the field. At the very moment I reached James, Martin Bayfield won a line-out cleanly, Dewi Morris whipped out a fast pass and Rob Andrew dropped that superb left-footed goal.

I could say that from that moment I was confident of victory, but the truth is I was confident all along. When the All Blacks scored their try, we didn't panic. We continued to play good, controlled rugby and stuck to our game plan. The hallmark of a great side is their ability to keep cool and not to panic under pressure. Look at the 1987 World Cup winners, New Zealand, or the Australian side in the 1991 World Cup. These were marvellous teams which never panicked under pressure, and in Wellington the Lions showed that they were also a great side.

Gavin Hastings kicked his third penalty early in the second half and his fourth near the end. In between came the best moment of the match. We had talked in team meetings and in training about how you might only get one chance to score a try in a Test match and it might not even be that obvious a chance, but you have to be ready and you have to take it. Twenty minutes into the second half that chance, or to be accurate, that half-chance came.

The All Blacks were using the rolling maul quite effectively after the interval and had, on this occasion, driven us back into our half

about 15 metres from the touchline. Sean Fitzpatrick broke away from the maul but dropped the ball. The Lions instantaneously sensed the opportunity to launch a blistering counter-attack. Dewi Morris scooped up the ball on his own ten-metre line, darted forward, straightening his run and flicking the ball on to Jeremy Guscott at the same time. Jerry burst up to halfway, eluding Frank Bunce with a swift injection of pace, and by just leaning in towards the middle of the field he forced John Kirwan to check for a split second. As Kirwan checked, Jerry passed to Rory Underwood, who was exploding up the touchline. Had the pass been a fraction earlier, Kirwan would have had time to turn into Rory, and had it been a fraction later it would have missed him. It

was executed to perfection. Rory accelerated down the touchline and past the flailing arms of John Timu to dive over in the corner for a truly spectacular try. From the moment Rory took the ball on the halfway line it was always going to be a try, but no praise can be too high for the fast reactions and supreme confidence of Guscott and Underwood as they weaved their magic under pressure in a very confined space.

The cheering from the 500 Gulliver's Travel supporters, all decked out in red, white and blue anoraks, reverberated round the ground. I always remember the Gulliver's Travel supporters lining up to form a guard of honour

at the Hyatt Hotel in Sydney after we won the Third Test and the series against Australia in 1989, and here they were roaring the team on again. The noise from the British supporters was fantastic and I made a mental note to tell the Gulliver's managing director, John Hall, that for the next Lions tour we would appreciate supporters from the start and then we

The final whistle and a record win. Pleasure for Ben Clarke and fans alike. Throughout the tour the players were very popular with the New Zealand crowds

wouldn't lose the First Test, as we did in 1989 and 1993!

In retrospect it is hard to pinpoint any one phase of the game or any one player who won the match for the Lions. It was a combination of all sorts of things. The line-out was a huge success. Martin Johnson did very well at the front, Martin Bayfield reigned supreme in the middle and stamped his presence all over the match and Ben Clarke was outstanding at the back with a little help from Dean Richards. Our scrummaging was excellent. Our loose play was even better; our recycling of the loose ball half a dozen times in rapid succession was an object lesson in our new, dynamic style of rugby. Winterbottom, Richards and Clarke were magnificent both in attack and defence. Perhaps, above all, our tackling was the most dramatic aspect of our performance. Not just the backs and the back row, but every one of the team. Popplewell, Moore and Leonard each had several priceless tackles in open play. So too did Johnson and Bayfield. At half-back Andrew and Morris tackled themselves to a standstill and I can't think of any pair of half-backs who have got through so much tackling in an international and done it with such relish. It was just like having an extra pair of flankers on the pitch for the whole match.

I would also argue that they played their best ever game of international rugby as a partnership. Throughout the game

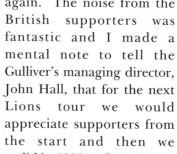

they kept taking the right options and Andrew's kicking was outstanding. Gibbs and Guscott tackled and covered all afternoon and their midfield defence must have broken the spirit of the All Blacks. The same applies to Rory Underwood and Ieuan Evans, and Ieuan can take comfort in the fact that he was not the only one to find Tuigamala a real handful and a half. And what can I say about Gavin Hastings? He was the inspiration behind everything and enjoyed yet another great Test match. He is a player who generates confidence and throughout the Lions tour he played tremendous rugby. He came on the tour as the best full-back in the world and played like it and proved it for eight weeks. But, in the final analysis, this triumph was not about any one player; it was a great team performance. The series was level. There was everything to play for in Auckland.

Back in the Test series with a vengeance. One of the most satisfying games of Lions rugby in which I have been involved.

The top players have a number of things in common.

Experience of playing conditions around the world. A capacity to read the game. A sense of teamwork. Strength. Speed. And, above all, the ability to make fast decisions.

HongkongBank

The Hongkong and Shanghai Banking Corporation Limited

A GAME TOO FAR
THE THIRD TEST MATCH

On the Sunday we flew to Hamilton for the penultimate game of the tour against Waikato, which would have been a difficult match for our Test side and proved an almost impossible task for the midweek team. Waikato were the reigning provincial champions and in the same class as Auckland, so I knew that nothing but our very best performance would be good enough.

The midweek side had flopped disastrously against Hawke's Bay and I hoped that they would be determined not to slip from grace two weeks in a row. It is easy to say that no one should need to be motivated to play for the British

Lions, but I can understand that the players had to deal with several conflicting emotions during the final week of the tour. The stark reality was that, rightly or wrongly, with the exception of Will Carling, the midweek players all felt that they had no real chance of making the Test team and therefore the biggest single incentive to produce the best was missing.

As they prepared for their final game it was hard not to be thinking of going home and I think quite a lot of them were mentally tired. They were up against an extremely strong side and they had no extra incentive to perform heroics because, come what may, this would be the end of their tour. I had assumed that as it was going to be their final match in a British Lions jersey they would all make a special effort but that did not happen. In the event, Carling had another excellent match and there were good performances from Anthony Clement and Tony

One of Waikato's well-worked tries.

Underwood in the backs and from Kenny Milne and Mike Teague in the pack. With only a third of the team playing really well, we were never in a challenging position and, for one reason or another, several of the players who had performed so well earlier in the tour failed to produce their best form on this occasion and we crashed to our biggest defeat of the trip.

We conceded three tries in the first half to turn around trailing by 26 points to 3. Waikato scored another two in the second half to win by 38–10. Will

Carling scored the Lions' only try and, captaining the side for the first time on the tour, he had an outstanding match, leading by example. However, Waikato had benefited from all their matches in the Super–10 competition and even though they did not have many exceptional individuals in their side, they did perform particularly well as a team. On this occasion, as against Hawke's Bay in Napier, the Lions did not.

Back in Auckland we began our preparations for the Third Test. Everyone knew this would be the toughest match of the whole tour, both mentally and

The centre pairings of Guscott and Gibbs (right) and Stensness and Bunce at practice before the crucial Third Test. Jeremy Guscott is running marginally straighter!

physically, and we were only too well aware that the All Blacks would come at us at 100 miles an hour to salvage their reputation. To prepare the Lions, I tried to work out what the All Blacks would try to do. In the Second Test the biggest single area which gave us control, and ultimately victory, was our domination of the line-out. It did not take a genius to work out that they would spend a great deal of time and energy making sure this did not happen again.

I was not the slightest bit surprised to learn that they had called in former All Black lock forward Andy Haden to help them sort out their line-out deficiencies. I suppose his advice would have been pretty predictable, but because he was one of the very best line-out players of the past 20 years, it would have carried a lot of authority and weight and the current New Zealand forwards would accept his word as gospel. Haden knew that they could not expect to outjump Martin Bayfield in a straight up and down jumping contest, one against one. Lesson number one was simply not to allow our line-out to be a straight jump between Jones and Bayfield. I anticipated this reaction but it was still going to be difficult to protect Bayfield.

The All Blacks practised exactly the opposite of what they had been preaching all through the tour – that there should be one metre between each player in the line and one metre between the two teams. Instead, in the Third Test, they deliberately crowded Bayfield and closed the line as the ball was being thrown in to put intense pressure on him. It worked perfectly for them after the initial concession of a couple of penalties. As the ball was thrown in, all seven New Zealand forwards took half a pace simultaneously towards our forwards and at precisely the same time the players immediately behind and in

front of Bayfield would impede him as well, of course, as Ian Jones or Mark Cooksley, the player in direct opposition.

We tried in practice on the Wednesday and Thursday to combat this possibility by giving Bayfield as much protection as we possibly could. Although this often allowed him to still get first touch of the ball in the Test, it did not give us the real quality ball we won in the Second Test and

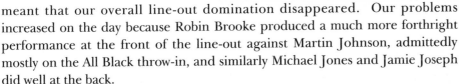

meant that our overall line-out domination disappeared. Our problems increased on the day because Robin Brooke produced a much more forthright performance at the front of the line-out against Martin Johnson, admittedly mostly on the All Black throw-in, and similarly Michael Jones and Jamie Joseph did well at the back.

Dean Richards, Peter Winterbottom and Dewi Morris work a blind-side move.

Again, one way to cut down the number of line-outs the Lions win in a Test on their own throw-in is simply to cut down the number of times they throw in. This is precisely what we predicted in training and precisely what happened at Eden Park. Of course, it is one thing to anticipate it, another to do something about it. The All Blacks decided not to kick to touch except in emergency situations as a last resort. Preston and Fox at half-back and Timu at full-back did exactly what we did in the Second Test so successfully – they kicked into that area over their forwards between the five-metre line and the touchline in defensive situations and into the middle of the field in attacking situations, but not to touch. If we cleared to touch they would have the throw and would be in a position to bunch up and crowd the front of the line to help Brooke win the ball or use Jones and Joseph at the back.

Preston and Fox kicked just as skilfully as Andrew and Morris had the previous week to secure victory for the Lions, and with much more of the ball the All Blacks were in the driving seat. Almost all of their tactical kicking was such that just as Rory Underwood and Ieuan Evans caught the ball they were tackled by their opposite numbers and driven backwards or forced into touch. In this way, New Zealand turned the game around with a complete transformation of their forward play in just seven days. First of all, they threw in to the line-out far more in Auckland than they had done in Wellington, and secondly, on our ball, they crowded the jumper and usually double-jumped. By that I mean that as the middle jumper took on his opposite number, the player one behind the New Zealand middle jumper also lurched forward towards the ball, making sure he made life as difficult as possible for our jumper.

By the second half we had sorted out the line-out difficulties but by then the All Blacks were in command. Our problems multiplied because in stark contrast to the Second Test we were outscrummaged in the Third Test; not badly, but just enough to give them the edge and make back-row moves and scrum-half breaking very difficult. Furthermore, being edged back in the scrums and outjumped in the line-out, we were inevitably going to struggle in the loose. The All Blacks had the better forward platform in the set pieces and that gave them the initiative in the open.

They played like men possessed and seldom can an All Blacks side ever have displayed more ferocious determination to win. We had the burning ambition in Wellington; they had it in Auckland. Their captain, Sean Fitzpatrick, told me that the week between the Second and Third Tests was without question the worst any of the New Zealand players could remember, and they were all ruthlessly committed to saving their reputations. They drove that fraction more aggressively, more abrasively, in the loose and although we still tackled really well, the extra intensity and power of the All Black forward machine meant they made an extra yard or sometimes half a yard in the tackle. We still kept putting in the "hits" all over the field but they were not always the big hits we managed in Wellington, and that was the crucial difference.

Lee Stensness in his first Test moves the ball positively in attack – a very good debut for him.

Tackling against a side playing for its life is very hard and these All Blacks knew it was make or break time. By gaining that vitally significant yard or half-yard as they kept driving at us, they were suddenly able to play the game one yard our side of the gain-line. That immediately made the game ten times easier for them and ten times harder for us. I mentioned this earlier but it is well worth emphasising again because it proved decisive in the Test series. In the Second Test we succeeded in defending our gain-line but in the Third Test, mainly because the All Blacks won more set-piece ball and had the advantage at the rucks and mauls, too often they were able to play the game on our side of the gain-line.

What is more, in Auckland they switched from the rolling mauls they had produced in Wellington to the far more effective traditional New Zealand rucking. Just as we had done in Wellington, they managed to win half a dozen rucks in succession, recycling the ball and hammering away at our defence. The Third Test was played at a faster pace but because we were unable to win as much possession as we had done in Wellington, we were thwarted in our attempt to play an expansive running game. I wanted to use the silky running of Jeremy Guscott, the cutting edge of Scott Gibbs, the powerful creativity of Gavin Hastings and the genuine speed of Rory Underwood and Ieuan Evans. They came into the game in the second half, but usually from defensive positions, and although they produced plenty of exciting running, the All Black defence managed to cope.

They also seemed keen to speed the game up and it was easier for them to dictate the pace, because they had more of the ball. What I did find ironic was the fact that after two indifferent performances in the first two Tests, for which they received a lot of criticism in the media, the All Blacks happily adopted the tactics in the Third Test that we had used in the Second. It was scarcely original thinking but I suppose we can take some satisfaction from the fact that we forced them to rethink their whole tactical approach and to change from the way that they had been playing to copy exactly what we were doing. In the Third Test they took us on at our style of play and I dare say we should take that as a compliment.

There is no doubt this was an exceptionally good All Black display and they deserved their victory, although I would suggest that the winning margin flattered them. We were able to withstand their initial forward onslaught and throughout the three-Test series I was never really concerned on the few occasions the All Blacks spun the ball along the threequarter line because I was absolutely confident that we could, man for man, mark them out of the game. They, in turn, acknowledged all through the tour that this was a very good British Lions side, and it was interesting that we were regularly compared to the 1971 Lions. Perhaps the most frustrating aspect of the last Test was the fact that it confirmed once again that there was very little between the two sides. That final Test, and with it the whole series, was balanced on a knife edge, the big difference being that the All Blacks grabbed all three of their scoring opportunities to collect 21 points while we created half a dozen try-scoring chances and managed to score only once.

Whatever the game in New Zealand you have to be ready for physical contact, and Ben Clarke is ready to meet the challenge of Craig Dowd.

Scott Gibbs scores the first try of the Third Test, and after all the pressure we get the points we wanted.

Nonetheless that try, which followed a Gavin Hastings penalty, gave us a 10-0 lead. From good rucked possession, Rob Andrew switched the ball inside to Rory Underwood on the burst. As he was stopped, the ball bounced off Frank Bunce towards the New Zealand line, where Scott Gibbs pounced to score. Unfortunately, in the next few minutes we gave away two tries which Fox converted and that meant we turned round 14–10 down. Having said that our midfield defence of Andrew, Gibbs and Guscott was virtually impenetrable, Stensness did push a kick over our threequarters into space and with the help of a kind bounce Bunce scored.

A few minutes later, a series of All Black forward drives led to a try from Fitzpatrick. In the first quarter of an hour of the second half Fox kicked two penalties and Hastings one to give New Zealand a lead of 20-13. We then came close to scoring twice and had several excellent attacks from deep defence, but the killer blow came 15 minutes from the end. Three scrums near our line produced three great attacking thrusts from the All Blacks. We contained the first two but not the third. Preston was released on the blind side and he darted outside Dean Richards and inside Gavin Hastings to score the winning try.

That gave the Test and the series to New Zealand. In retrospect our chance of taking the series was probably lost when we failed to win the First Test in Christchurch. We came tantalisingly close that day, and if we had held on to our lead in those dying minutes I am certain we would have won one of the two remaining Tests.

Instead, we were left with an almost impossible task of having to win both

John Preston shows the ball to John Kirwan and then takes the gap for New Zealand's crucial third try.

remaining Tests. No team since the Australians in 1949 has managed to beat the All Blacks twice in succession in New Zealand. The Lions have never achieved such a feat in history, not even the 1971 Lions. We failed and all credit to Laurie Mains, their coach, and Sean Fitzpatrick, their captain. But I know and I like to think they probably would also admit that if there had been a Fourth Test the following Saturday it would have been absolutely evenly balanced. I truly believe that the 1993 Lions were every bit as good as the All Blacks and I would certainly have backed us to win if there had been another Test.

But that, of course, is pure conjecture. At the end of eight memorable weeks in New Zealand we had played some very good rugby in the big matches, we had presented the All Blacks with a real challenge and we had taken the series to the wire. We had made a host of friends on and off the field and I reckon we had been very good ambassadors. The 1993 Lions were a very happy touring party and I was very proud to be part of them. I only wish we could have won that Final Test but at least the victory in the Second Test in Wellington will remain one of the really great highlights of my rugby career. Any victory over the All Blacks is a prize to be treasured. I dare say that the epitaph for the 1993 British Lions will simply read – they came so close to glory.

The faces say it all. The players have given everything but we are desperately disappointed to miss out on the series.

A series completed, now it's time to swap jerseys and to reflect on what might have been.

A warm welcome from Qantas on the homeward journey
helped to take my mind off what might have been.

REFLECTIONS
FINAL THOUGHTS FROM GAVIN HASTINGS

How did you see your role as captain and how did touring with the British Lions in 1989 help you?

First of all, I think the fact that I was a member of the 1989 Lions tour to Australia was a considerable advantage to me because I learned on that trip how to cope with a two-month tour instead of the normal one-month trip, which is the maximum each individual country goes for. It is a long time to be away, changing hotels and towns twice a week for the best part of eight weeks, and I appreciated that there was a danger of some guys losing interest if things

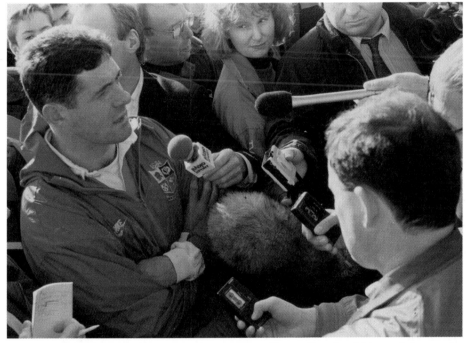

Gavin giving one of his cosy press conferences at the end of a training session.

were not going well either for them personally or for the Lions. I knew the feeling in Australia of losing the First Test after an unbeaten provincial run, which is almost exactly what happened in New Zealand, and I knew how really important it was to approach every day in a very positive frame of mind. It is the captain's job to convey that sense of urgency and that positive attitude to ensure that all 30 players are not only happy and enjoying the tour but that they all share a burning ambition to win every match. I am sure this helped us to win the Second Test in both Australia and New Zealand, and to keep the series alive in each case until the very last match. It is amazing how similar my two Lions tours have been and there is no doubt that being on the first helped me on the second. I think this year's tour was an extremely happy one, with things going very well until the last ten days when the players in the midweek side, with the exception of Will Carling, all knew that at that point they had virtually no chance of a Test place and the major extra incentive of hitting peak form was missing. Up until then all 30 players had worked flat out to the maximum of their potential and if the tour had ended after the Second Test it would have been regarded as a real success.

What were the biggest disappointments of the tour?

The biggest single disappointment was unquestionably losing the last Test because we knew we were good enough to win and a victory would have put us right up there as one of the best ever Lions teams. Defeat meant we were just another British side who came close to glory but did not quite make it. Of course, if we had won the First Test we would have won the series anyway; my second biggest disappointment was watching the referee award New Zealand the penalty in the very last minute, for no obvious reason, which deprived the Lions of a certain victory. It was a shattering experience summed up by the look of utter bewilderment on Dewi Morris's face as he was certain the referee was going to award the penalty to us. It was the most controversial decision of the entire tour and probably of my international rugby career, but although we all felt very hard done by we did not let it break our resolve and we came back to win the Second Test. The other general disappointments were the performances of the midweek side in their final two matches against Hawke's Bay and Waikato. They lost both badly and failed to do themselves justice, but against that, they had all put in some very good displays earlier in the tour.

What were the main highlights of the tour?

There's no doubt that the main high point of the trip was winning the Second Test in Wellington. I think it is very important to put into perspective just what an achievement that was. I have played four times for Scotland against New Zealand and lost every time. In fact, Scotland have never beaten the All Blacks. I have also played in losing teams for Edinburgh, the Barbarians, a Japanese President's XV and two World XVs against New Zealand. Add in two defeats for the Lions and in 11 matches against New Zealand I have only twice been on the winning side – the first match for the World XV in 1992 and the Second Test for the British Lions in 1993. The All Blacks are the benchmark in international rugby and to beat them in a Test is the greatest possible thrill and achievement for the entire Lions squad. I think I am right in saying that the only member of our party who had previously been on a winning side against New Zealand was Peter Winterbottom, for England at Twickenham in 1983. But he knew the other side of the coin, because that same year he had been in the British Lions side which had lost all four Tests in New Zealand. In Wellington, we produced 80 minutes of outstanding rugby of the very highest class to win convincingly and comprehensively. We planned a major tactical operation which demanded great control, discipline, concentration and skill and we executed that plan to perfection. The All Blacks were devastated and it is hard to exaggerate the tremendous feeling of satisfaction every British Lion experienced right through the game and on the final whistle. We dominated the line-out, our tactical kicking from Rob Andrew and Dewi Morris was virtually faultless, the forwards were fearless in the loose and our tackling was phenomenal. The icing on the cake came with Rory Underwood's try. This was made with a flash of genius from Jerry Guscott which I doubt any of the All Blacks could have matched, drawing the defence and timing the pass to the absolute split second which allowed Rory Underwood to use his blistering speed to score. That was probably the best single moment of the tour. The other highlights came early on in the first three games. It was good that all 30 players took part in the first two games and against strong opposition they played really well to win their first match in a British Lions jersey on the tour. The style of both these wins against North Auckland and North Harbour was extremely encouraging. And perhaps the second most satisfying victory came in the third match when we recovered from 20–0 down to beat the Maoris 24-20 with a storming performance in the final 20 minutes, when we scored three exciting tries. That game was also played in Wellington, so I have to say that that was my favourite city in 1993.

The Lions lost the series 2-1 but did you feel the All Blacks were the better team?

No, I definitely did not. I honestly thought the two teams were very evenly matched and the series was always going to be decided by a couple of things suddenly going right for one team at a crucial moment. If you look back on the series the facts speak for themselves. The Lions won one Test decisively, the All Blacks won one Test decisively and the other Test went to the All Blacks in the last minute of the match, when we were deservedly leading 18-17 after a magnificent second half performance, until the referee, for no apparent reason, awarded a penalty to New Zealand which Grant Fox kicked from near the halfway line. When you remember that the All Blacks were also given an extremely controversial try in the opening minute of the Test, it is very difficult to escape the feeling that we were very unfortunate not to win the First Test and certainly, on the day, I believe we outplayed New Zealand. If you accept that we were much the better side in the Second Test, I really believe that if we had played a fourth Test one week after the Third, we would have been good enough to win. The whole of our Test team were confident that we were every bit as good as the All Blacks and would have had a tremendous chance of sharing a four-Test series. I don't believe for a moment that British rugby, playing collectively as the Lions, is in any way inferior to New Zealand rugby.

If you take the major individual countries in 1993 what do you think the world pecking order is?

I would begin by not answering that particular question but by saying that after the British Lions had won the Test series against Australia in 1989, and after the Wallabies went on to win the World Cup in 1991, and after our showing on the Lions tour in 1993, British rugby is as good as that of any country in the world. But I have to say that it is the sum of the four individual parts and not those parts on their own. I think everyone would accept that Australia and New

Zealand are the top at the moment and they are both well clear of any other single country. With the one-off Bledisloe Cup match in Dunedin in July going to New Zealand, I would place them at the very top followed by Australia. Without any hesitation I would place England in third spot and all the other countries would be some way adrift. England did, after all, provide 11 of the Lions Test team. I would then tend to bracket Scotland, France and South Africa together in joint fourth, but if I had to split them up I would put France fourth, Scotland fifth and South Africa sixth on everything they had achieved up to the middle of 1993. France did win the Five Nations Championship, with Scotland second, and France did beat the Springboks, albeit very narrowly, in their Test series in South Africa. There would be very little between Ireland and Wales but I would place Ireland seventh and Wales eighth.

With the hectic fixture schedule growing ever more crowded there is a feeling that the Lion is an endangered species. Do you think British Lions tours should continue?

Categorically, and emphatically, yes. If I had to pick out the three highlights of my rugby career I would select without any hesitation my two British Lions tours and Scotland's Grand Slam in 1990. The very fact that the two Lions tours feature so prominently in my memory underlines just how important they are to me and every player who has represented the Lions. It is the ultimate honour for any British rugby player, and playing in a Test for the Lions is the greatest experience I have had. You only have to ask the players who toured New Zealand in 1993 what their biggest challenge and accolade in rugby was and they would all say it was representing the British Lions. Individually, each Home Union country has an extremely limited chance of beating New Zealand in a Test, but collectively all things are possible, as we proved in Wellington. Look at it this way. Scotland and Ireland have never beaten New Zealand, home or away, in history, and between England and Wales, only once have England beaten the All Blacks in New Zealand. On that basis, you can understand how much the New Zealanders look forward to a British Lions tour and how, by comparison, they can never get nearly so excited about a tour by just one single Home Union. In one case, they know they face a real challenge, in the other they know they are more or less certain of victory. This year's tour was a huge success for New Zealand, with enormous crowds turning up for all the provincial matches and three capacity gates for the three Tests. Believe me, I have played over 50 games of international rugby and I have found nothing so exciting, nerve-racking, full of tension and a real buzz as playing a Test match for the British Lions against the New Zealand All Blacks. And I know I speak for every Lion who has ever done that down through the pages of history. It is a very, very special occasion and one that I will cherish and savour always. As far as I am concerned I would not have swapped my eight weeks as captain of the British Lions for anything. It was the trip of a lifetime, a tour to a rugby-mad nation, never to be forgotten. I wish we had won the Test series but at least we gave it our very best shot and we came very close. Long live Lions tours.

TOUR DETAILS

THE LIONS IN NEW ZEALAND, MAY - JULY 1993

APPEARANCES

+ Denotes replacement appearance.
Figures in brackets denote Test appearances.
* Denotes tour replacement after commencement.
Figures are in order of first appearance.

BACKS
A. Clement Swansea/Wales 6+1;
I. Hunter Northampton/England 1;
S. Hastings Watsonians/Scotland 2+1;
J. Guscott Bath/England 7+2 (3);
R. Underwood Leicester/RAF/England 7 (3);
S. Barnes Bath/England 6+2;
R. Jones Swansea/Wales 6;
G. Hastings Watsonians/Scotland 8+1 (3);
I. Evans Llanelli/Wales 7 (3);
W. Carling Harlequins/England 6+1 (1);
S. Gibbs Swansea/Wales 7 (2);
T. Underwood Leicester/England 6;
R. Andrew Wasps/England 7 (3);
D. Morris Orrel/Englandl 7+1 (3);
*R. Wallace Garryowen/Ireland 5;
*V. Cunningham St. Mary's College/Ireland 3;
*A. Nicol Dundee High School FP/Scotland 0+1.

FORWARDS England caps unless stated
J. Leonard Harlequins/England 7+1 (2);
B. Moore Harlequins/England 7 (2);
P. Wright Boroughmuir/Scotland 6;
M. Galwey Shannon/Ireland 6+1;
D. Cronin London Scottish/Scotland 6;
 A. Reed Bath/Scotland 6 (1);
R. Webster Swansea/Wales 6+1;
B. Clarke Bath/England 7+1 (3);
N. Popplewell Greystones/Ireland 7 (3);
K. Milne Heriot's FP/Scotland 6+1 (1);
P. Burnell London Scottish/Scotland 6 (1);
M. Teague Moseley/England 7;
M. Bayfield Northampton/England 7 (3);
W. Dooley Preston Grasshoppers/England 3;
P. Winterbottom Harlequins/England 7 (3);
D. Richards Leicester/England 6 (3);
*M. Johnson Leicester/England 4 (2).

SCORERS (All matches)

G. Hastings (1 try, 24 pens., 12 cons.) 101 pts.; S. Barnes (7 pens, 6 cons.) 33 pts.; R. Andrew (2 tries, 2 d.g., 2 pens., 1 con.) 24 pts.; I Evans (4 tries) 20 pts.; R. Underwood (3 tries) 15 pts.; A. Clement (2 tries, 1 d.g.) 13 pts.; J. Guscott (2 tries) 10 pts.; T Underwood (2 tries) 10 pts.; R. Webster (2 tries) 10 pts.; V. Cunningham (2 tries) 10 pts., S. Gibbs (2 tries) 10 pts.; W. Carling (1 try, 1 d.g.) 8 pts.; S. Hastings (1 try) 5 pts.; M. Galwey (1 try) 5 pts.; D. Richards (1 try) 5 pts.; A. Reed (1 try) 5 pts.; R. Wallace (1 try) 5 pts.; 2 penalty tries - 10 pts.

SCORERS (Test Matches)

G. Hastings (12 pens, 1 con.) 38 pts.; R. Underwood (1 try) 5 pts.; S. Gibbs (1 try) 5 pts.; R. Andrew (1 d.g.) 3 pts.

RESULTS

v North Auckland	Whangarei	W	30–17
v North Harbour	Mount Smart Stadium, Auckland	W	29–13
v New Zealand Maoris	Wellington	W	24–20
v Canterbury	Christchurch	W	28–10
v Otago	Dunedin	L	24–37
v Southland	Invercargill	W	34–16
v New Zealand (1st Test)	Christchurch	L	18–20
v Taranaki	New Plymouth	W	49–25
v Auckland	Eden Park, Auckland	L	18–23
v Hawke's Bay	Napier	L	17–29
v New Zealand (2nd Test)	Wellington	W	20–7
v Waikato	Hamilton	L	10–38
v New Zealand (3rd Test)	Eden Park, Auckland	L	13–30

NORTH AUCKLAND 17 BRITISH ISLES 30

North Auckland: W. Johnston; T. Going, C. Going,
M. Seymour, D. Manako, A. Monaghan, R. Le Bas,
L. Davies, D. Te Puni, C. Barrell, G. Taylor, I. Jones captain,
E. Jones, A. Going, K. Tuipolotu.

REPLACEMENTS: R. Hilton-Jones for Tuipolotu 59 minutes,
L. Sigley for Te Puni 77 minutes

British Isles: A. Clement, I. Hunter, S. Hastings, J. Guscott,
R. Underwood, S. Barnes captain, R. Jones, J. Leonard,
B. Moore, P. Wright, M. Galwey, D. Cronin, A. Reed,
R. Webster, B. Clarke.

REPLACEMENT: G. Hastings for Hunter 38 minutes

REFEREE: L. McLachlan, Otago

SCORERS
NORTH AUCKLAND: Te Puni 1 try, Seymour 1 try, T. Going
1 try, Johnston 1 con.
BRITISH ISLES: Guscott 1 try, S. Hastings 1 try, Clement 1 try,
R. Underwood 1 try, Barnes 1 pen., 1 con., G. Hastings 1
pen., 1 con.

HALF-TIME: 12-15

NORTH HARBOUR 13 BRITISH ISLES 29

North Harbour: I. Calder, E. Rush, F. Bunce, W. Little,
R. Kapa, J. Carter, A. Strachan, R. Williams, G. Dowd,
K. Boroevich, A. Perelini, B. Larsen, D. Mayhew, L. Barry,
R. Turner captain.

REPLACEMENT: R. George for Larsen 78 minutes

British Isles: G. Hastings captain, I. Evans, W. Carling,
S. Gibbs, T. Underwood, R. Andrew, D. Morris,
N. Popplewell, K. Milne, P. Burnell, M. Teague,
M. Bayfield, W. Dooley, P. Winterbottom, D. Richards.

REPLACEMENT: R. Webster for Richards 55 minutes

REFEREE: A. Riley, Waikato

SCORERS
NORTH HARBOUR: Perelini 1 try, Carter 2 pens., 1 con.
BRITISH ISLES: Andrew 1 try, T. Underwood 1 try, Evans 1 try,
Webster 1 try, G. Hastings 1 pen., 3 cons.

HALF-TIME:: 6-15

NZ MAORIS 20 BRITISH ISLES 24

New Zealand Maoris: S. Doyle, E. Rush, G. Konia,
R. Ellison, A. Price, S. Hirini, S. Forster, G. Hurunui,
N. Hewitt, K. Boroevich, J. Joseph, J. Coe, M. Cooksley,
Z. Brooke, A. Pene captain.

British Isles: G. Hastings captain, I. Evans, S. Hastings,
W. Carling, R. Underwood, S. Barnes, D. Morris,
N. Popplewell, B. Moore, P. Wright, M. Teague, D. Cronin,
W. Dooley, P. Winterbottom, B. Clarke.

REPLACEMENTS: J. Leonard for Popplewell 51 minutes,
J. Guscott for Carling 75 minutes

REFEREE: G. Lempriere, Manawatu

SCORERS
NEW ZEALAND MAORIS:
Prince 1 try, Hirini 1 try, 2 pens., 2 cons.
BRITISH ISLES: Evans 1 try, R. Underwood 1 try, G. Hastings
1 try, 1 pen., 3 cons.

HALF-TIME: 20-0

CANTERBURY 10 BRITISH ISLES 28

Canterbury: A. Lawry, P. Bale, S. Philpott, K. Hansen,
S. Cleave, G. Coffey, G. Bachop, G. Halford, M. Hammett,
S. Loe, T. Blackadder, C. England, M. McAtamney,
G. Smith, R. Penney captain

REPLACEMENTS: W. Maunsell for Hansen 4 minutes,
T. Kele for Halford 63 minutes

British Isles: A. Clement, R. Wallace, S. Gibbs, J. Guscott,
T. Underwood, R. Andrew, R. Jones, J. Leonard, K. Milne,
P. Burnell, M. Galwey, M. Bayfield, A. Reed, B. Clarke,
D. Richards captain

REPLACEMENT: S. Barnes for Andrew 79 minutes

REFEREE: J. Taylor, Counties

SCORERS
CANTERBURY: Smith 1 try, Coffey 1 pen., 1 con.,
BRITISH ISLES: Guscott 1 try, Galwey 1 try, T. Underwood
1 try, Andrew 1 try, 1 d.g., 1 pen., 1 con.

HALF-TIME: 7-8

OTAGO 37 BRITISH ISLES 24

Otago: J. Timu, A. Bell, M. Ellis, J. Leslie, P. Cooke,
S. Bachop, S. Forster, R. Moore, D. Latta captain, M. Mika,
J. Kronfeld, A. Rich, G. MacPherson, J. Joseph, A. Pene

British Isles: G. Hastings captain, I. Evans, W. Carling,
J. Guscott, R. Underwood, S. Barnes, D. Morris,
N. Popplewell, K. Milne, P. Burnell, M. Teague, W. Dooley,
M. Bayfield, P. Winterbottom, D. Richards.

REPLACEMENTS: S. Hastings for Carling 9 minutes, A. Clement
for S. Hastings 47 minutes, M. Galwey for Bayfield 79
minutes

REFEREE: C. Hawke, South Canterbury

SCORERS:
OTAGO: Cooke 2 tries, leslie 1 try, Latta 1 try, Timu 1 try, Bachop 1 d.g., Bell 1 pen., 3 cons
BRITISH ISLES: Richards 1 try, Evans 1 try, G. Hastings 4 pens., 1 con.

HALF-TIME:: 13-18

SOUTHLAND 16 BRITISH ISLES 34

SOUTHLAND
S. Forrest, P. Johnston, A. James, G. Beardsley, J. Cormack, S. Culhane, B. Murrell, R. Palmer, D. Heaps, C. Corbett, B. Morton, M. Tinnock, W. Millar, P. henderson captain, R. Smith

REPLACEMENTS: D. Henderson for P. Henderson 40 minutes, R. Bekhuis for Tinnock 74 minutes

British Isles: G. Hastings captain, R. Wallace, S. Gibbs, A. Clement, T. Underwood, R. Andrew, R. Jones, J. Leonard, B. Moore, P. Wright, M. Teague, D. Cronin, A. Reed, R. Webster, M. Galwey

REPLACEMENTS: S. Barnes for Andrew 67 minutes, J. Guscott for Gibbs 69 minutes, D. Morris for Barnes 79 minutes

REFEREE: M. Fitzgibbon, Canterbury

SCORERS
SOUTHLAND: Cormack 1 try, Johnston 1 try, Culhane 2 pens.
BRITISH ISLES: Reed 1 try, Clement 1 try, 1 d.g., 1 penalty try, G. Hastings 4 pens., 2 cons.

HALF-TIME:: 0-24

NEW ZEALAND 20 BRITISH ISLES 18
FIRST TEST

NEW ZEALAND Auckland unless stated
J. Timu (Otago); E. Clarke, F. Bunce (North Harbour), W. Little (North Harbour), V. Tuigamala, G. Fox, A. Strachan (North Harbour), C. Dowd, S. Fitzpatrick captain, O. Brown, J. Joseph (Otago), R. Brooke, I. Jones (North Auckland), M. Jones, Z. Brooke.

REPLACEMENT: M. Cooper (Waikato) for Little 79 minutes.

NEW CAP: Dowd.

British Isles: G. Hastings captain, I. Evans Wales, W. Carling,, J. Guscott, R Underwood, R. Andrew, D. Morris, N. Popplewell, K. Milne, P. Burnell, B. Clarke, M. Bayfield, A. Reed, P. Winterbottom, D. Richards

NEW BRITISH ISLESS CAPS: Carling, Morris, Popplewell, Milne, Burnell, Clarke, Bayfield, Reed

REFEREE: B. Kinsey, Australia

SCORERS
NEW ZEALAND: Bunce 1 try, Fox 5 pens.
BRITISH ISLES: G. Hastings 6 pens.

HALF-TIME: 11-9

TARANAKI 25 - BRITISH ISLES 49

TARANAKI
K. Crowley, D. Murfitt, K. Mahon, D. Eynon, A. Martin, J. Cameron, W. Dombroski, M. Allen captain, S. McDonald, G. Slater, A. Slater, B. O'Sullivan, J. Roache, F. Mahoni, N. Hill

British Isles: A. Clement, R. Wallace, V. Cunningham, S. Gibbs, T. Underwood, S. Barnes captain, R. Jones, P. Wright, B. Moore, J. Leonard, M. Teague, M. Johnson, D. Cronin, R. Webster, M. Galwey.

REPLACEMENTS: B. Clarke for Galwey 33 minutes, A. Nicol for Jones 76 minutes, K. Milne for Teague 76 minutes

REFEREE: S. Walsh Wellington

SCORERS
TARANAKI: O'Sullivan 1 try, A. Slater 1 try, McDonald 1try, Crowley 2 pens., 2 cons.
BRITISH ISLES: Cunningham 2 tries, Cronin 1 try, Teague 1 try, Jones 1 try, Wallace 1 try, Gibbs 1 try, Barnes 2 pens., 4 cons.

HALF-TIME: 13-20

AUCKLAND 23 - BRITISH ISLES 18

AUCKLAND
S. Howarth, J. Kirwan, W. Sututu, L. Stensness, E. Clarke, G. Fox, J. Hewett, C. Dowd, S. Fitzpatrick, O. Brown, B. Jackson, R. Brooke, R. Fromont, M. Jones, Z. Brooke captain

REPLACEMENT: C. Adams for Howarth 10 minutes

British Isles: G. Hastings captain, I. Evans, S. Gibbs, J. Guscott, R. Underwood, R. Andrew, D. Morris, N. Popplewell, B. Moore, P. Burnell, R. Webster, M. Johnson, M. Bayfield, P. Winterbottom, B. Clarke

REPLACEMENT: W. Carling for Hastings 40 minutes

TEMPORARY REPLACEMENT: K. Milne for Moore

REFEREE: D. Bishop Southland

SCORERS
AUCKLAND: Kirwan 1 try, Fox 6 pens.

BRITISH ISLES: Evans 1 try, 1 penalty try, G. Hastings 1 pen., 1 con., Andrew 1 pen.

HALF-TIME:: 11-18

HAWKE'S BAY 29 - BRITISH ISLES 17

Hawke's Bay: J. Cunningham, A. Hamilton, G. Konia, M. Paewai, P. Davis, S. Kerr, N. Weber, T. Taylor, N. Hewitt captain, O. Crawford, D. Watts, J. Fowler, W. Davison, G. Falcon, S. Tremain

British Isles: A. Clement, R. Wallace, V. Cunningham, W. Carling, T. Underwood, S. Barnes captain, R. Jones, P. Wright, K. Milne, J. Leonard, M. Teague, D. Cronin, A. Reed, R. Webster, M. Galwey

REFEREE: P. O'Brien North Otago

SCORERS
HAWKE'S BAY: Hewitt 1 try, Weber 1 try, Tremain 1 try, Kerr 1 d.g., 1 pen., 1 con., Cunningham 2 pens.
BRITISH ISLES: Webster 1 try, Carling 1 d.g., Barnes 3 pens.

Half-time: 5-17

NEW ZEALAND 7 - BRITISH ISLES 20
SECOND TEST

New Zealand: Auckland unless stated
J. Timu (Otago), J. Kirwan, E. Clarke, F. Bunce (North Harbour), V. Tuigamala, G. Fox, J. Preston (Wellington), C. Dowd, S. Fitzpatrick captain, O. Brown, J. Joseph (Otago), R. Brooke, M. Cooksley (Counties), M. Jones, Z. Brooke

NEW CAP: Cooksley

REPLACEMENT: I. Jones (North Auckland) for Cooksley 40 minutes

British Isles: G. Hastings captain, I. Evans, S. Gibbs, J. Guscott, R. Underwood, R. Andrew, D. Morris, N. Popplewell, B. Moore, J. Leonard, B. Clarke, M. Johnson, M. Bayfield, P. Winterbottom, D. Richards

NEW BRITISH ISLES CAPS: Gibbs, Leonard, Johnson

TEMPORARY REPLACEMENT: M. Teague for Winterbottom

REFEREE: P. Robin, France

SCORERS
NEW ZEALAND: Clarke 1 try, Fox 1 con.
BRITISH ISLES: R. Underwood 1 try, Andrew 1 d.g., G. Hastings 4 pens.

HALF-TIME:: 7-9

WAIKATO 38 - BRITISH ISLES 10

Waikato: M. Cooper, D. Wilson, A. Collins, R. Ellison, W. Warlow, I. Foster, S. Crabb, C. Stevenson, W. Gatland, G. Purvis, R. Jerram, S. Gordon, B. Anderson, D. Monkley, J. Mitchell captain

REPLACEMENT: M. Russell for Anderson 71 minutes

British Isles: A. Clement, R. Wallace, V. Cunningham, W. Carling captain, T. Underwood, S. Barnes, R. Jones, P. Wright, K. Milne, P. Burnell, M. Teague, D. Cronin, A. Reed, R. Webster, M. Galwey

REFEREE: T. Marshall, Canterbury

SCORERS
WAIKATO: Monkley 2 tries, Wilson 1 try, Collins 1 try, Gatland 1 try, Cooper 3 pens., 2 cons.
BRITISH ISLES: Carling 1 try, Barnes 1 pen., 1 con

HALF-TIME: 26-3

NEW ZEALAND 30 - BRITISH ISLES 13
THIRD TEST

New Zealand: Auckland unless stated
J. Timu (Otago), J. Kirwan, F. Bunce (North Harbour), L. Stensness, V. Tuigamala, G. Fox, J. Preston (Wellington), C. Dowd, S. Fitzpatrick captain, O. Brown, J. Joseph (Otago), I. Jones (North Auckland), R. Brooke, M. Jones, A. Pene (Otago)

REPLACEMENT: M. Cooksley (Counties) for I. Jones 20 minutes, Z. Brooke for M. Jones 74 minutes

TEMPORARY REPLACEMENT: M. Cooper (Waikato) twice for Timu

NEW CAP: Stensness

British Isles: G. Hastings captain, I. Evans, S. Gibbs, J. Guscott, R. Underwood, R. Andrew, D. Morris, N. Popplewell, B. Moore, J. Leonard, B. Clarke, M. Johnson, M. Bayfield, P. Winterbottom, D. Richards

NO NEW BRITISH ISLES CAPS

REFEREE: P. Robin, France

SCORERS
NEW ZEALAND: Bunce 1 try, Fitzpatrick 1 try, Preston 1 try, Fox 3 pens., 3 cons.
BRITISH ISLES: Gibbs 1 try, Hastings 2 pens., 1 con

HALF-TIME: 14-10